EDWARD WESSEX'S

CROWN
AND
COUNTRY

A Personal Guide to

ROYAL LONDON

EDWARD WESSEX'S
CROWN AND COUNTRY

A Personal Guide to

ROYAL LONDON

HarperCollins*Illustrated*

Ardent
PRODUCTIONS LIMITED

CARLTON

CONTENTS

INTRODUCTION

For more than a thousand years this country has had a monarchy. For at least eight hundred years our monarchs were the executive power in the land. Little was done without their consent. Although such power was total it was only achievable with co-operation and support from the majority. The monarchs only ruled with the consent of the people and thus they needed to develop a relationship with the country they reigned. *Crown and Country* explores that relationship, the many ways in which it works, what has resulted from it and the effects it has had over the centuries, most specifically in our capital city, London.

What makes London of particular interest is that it reflects both nationally important issues as well as local associations. The royal palaces and residences such as the Tower of London, Buckingham Palace or Hampton Court are nationally as well as internationally renowned. Many of the stories and legends recounted here will be instantly recognisable or at least appreciated beyond the local area. Yet in spite of this, it will be the character of London, its surrounding boroughs and the people who live here which will be most clearly reflected in the following pages, text and pictures.

London's relationship with the Crown is reflected in many more ways than just in its buildings. As with other parts of the country, there are legends, curious titles, local associations and public institutions all of which have close connections with the Crown. For instance, around London there is the legend of King John and the Silent Pool near Shere, how the Isle of Dogs acquired its curious name, what special role the Royal Watermen perform on the River Thames and why the Victoria & Albert Museum is so called. What appears from these myriad stories is how deeply the Crown is ingrained in our culture and heritage in countless way.

Perhaps the most obvious way the story of the Crown is inextricably linked with the life of our nation is through measuring time. The reigns of our kings and queens act as a timeline through history, providing clear reference points, reflecting periods, indicating changing styles and fashions. Talking about William the Conqueror immediately takes us back to the Norman invasion, Richard the Lionheart to the Crusades, Charles I to the Civil War, Queen Victoria to the industrial revolution and empire. Monarchs are also people, individuals who in their own way humanise our nation's story, and as such we can relate to them more than to some faceless bureaucratic machine or series of meaningless dates.

The other point about monarchs as individuals is that they have their own characteristics and personal interests. These are reflected in their actions and legacies, whether as warriors or administrators, builders or conservationists, innovators or traditionalists. Of course not all monarchs were brilliant, far from it, but given that we have left our choice of sovereign to destiny perhaps this is not that surprising. Inheritance through an accident of birth is never going to be a perfect method of selecting a leader, but it does in most cases produce a sense of continuity and reassurance. I say 'most cases' because there have been times when the succession has been in doubt (Elizabeth I had no children, nor did Queen Anne) or has been usurped by force (Edward IV, Richard III or Henry VII). In Queen Anne's case, a Parliamentary law insisting succession be to a protestant meant that the Elector of Hanover became King George I in spite of 57 other people having a better claim! Having said all that, the country hasn't done too badly. Yes, there have been some bad kings, some have been moderate and just got by, but there have been enough good ones to have got us to where we are today.

One thing *Crown and Country* does not try to do is tell the whole story of the Crown in London. This is not a history lesson, but an exploration of various places and the stories attached to them. Through these locations and stories we reflect the character of the place and people who lived and worked there. We will also explore the associations and connections these places and people have had with the Crown and so reveal the relationship.

The Crown in this sense means two things. The first is the person, the sovereign, the embodiment of the concept of nationality represented by the object of the Crown. The second is the administration which supports and represents the sovereign. Many things are enacted in the name of the Crown, as the embodiment of the ultimate authority in the land, from Acts of Parliament to appointments of key positions. It is worth remembering that nobody holds true authority in this country without the sanction of the monarch, whether they be government ministers, judges, bishops or generals. The powers they hold are delegated to them by the monarch who holds them in trust for the people, and these powers are only given on a temporary basis.

'Country' also has two meanings. In one sense we are talking about the country as a whole. More often we are talking about the local area – in this case London. There is no overall story of the capital, but through various episodes we will build a picture of London over the centuries – how it started out as a small village which the Celts called Llyn din or 'hill by the pool', was developed into a walled city by the Romans at the head of London Bridge, was made a capital by the Normans, became the commercial and financial centre of the kingdom, was virtually burnt to the ground, and how it has in the last 150 years grown so big that it has swallowed up the surrounding towns and villages. It's difficult to imagine now what this city must have looked like a mere two hundred years ago when there were no really tall buildings, there was a clear distinction between boroughs, the River Thames was nearly twice as wide and there were hardly any bridges. The country then was dominated by royal buildings. At one time there were nearly thirty in and around London, although the significant ones are the same now as then: Westminster Abbey, the Banqueting House of Whitehall Palace, the Tower of London and Greenwich Palace.

Many of these places reflect the interests of the monarchs who are associated with them. Westminster Abbey still contains the shrine of its original builder and saint, Edward the Confessor. The White Tower at the Tower of London was the original fortress built by William the Conqueror as part of his ring of defences around London, which also includes the castles at Hertford and Guildford. Henry VIII had the Astronomical Clock installed at Hampton Court. The magnificent Rubens' painted ceiling in the Banqueting House was commissioned by Charles I. Charles II was responsible for the Royal Observatory at Greenwich and appointed the first Astronomer Royal. These were all personal passions.

In their official role, monarchs were involved in building churches, supporting schools and colleges, issuing royal charters, calling and chairing parliaments, travelling the country and ensuring its defence, as well as a host of other activities. Although such activities were carried out the length and breadth of the kingdom, they were all commissioned in London. Several monarchs took an active interest in St Paul's Cathedral, particularly Charles II during the rebuilding by Christopher Wren which followed the Great Fire. Royal Watermen were and still are a special body of men whose job it is to convey the sovereign and members of the Royal Family along the Thames. The royal dockyards at Deptford became so famous that even the Tsar of Russia came to see how they operated. Royal Charters were specific methods of establishing organisations, giving them self-governing laws and clear trading guidelines or practices. The original trade monopolies or Livery Companies in the City were created this way and still abide by the same basic health and safety rules. When the sovereign wished to introduce new legislation, he or she would summon Parliament and state the agenda. Technically this could happen anywhere, but traditionally Parliament met at the Palace of Westminster. So each place or organisation has its own relationship with the Crown and vice versa.

These are just a few of the places and a few of the characters you will meet on our exploration of London. They are by no means a definitive list, but hopefully will give a sense of the many varied ways in which the Crown has evolved and developed its relationship with different parts of the capital. Perhaps it will also give readers a new appreciation of some of this city's great treasures, customs and traditions. Most importantly, I hope that it will be a book to which you will return time and time again to re-check a fact or re-read a story.

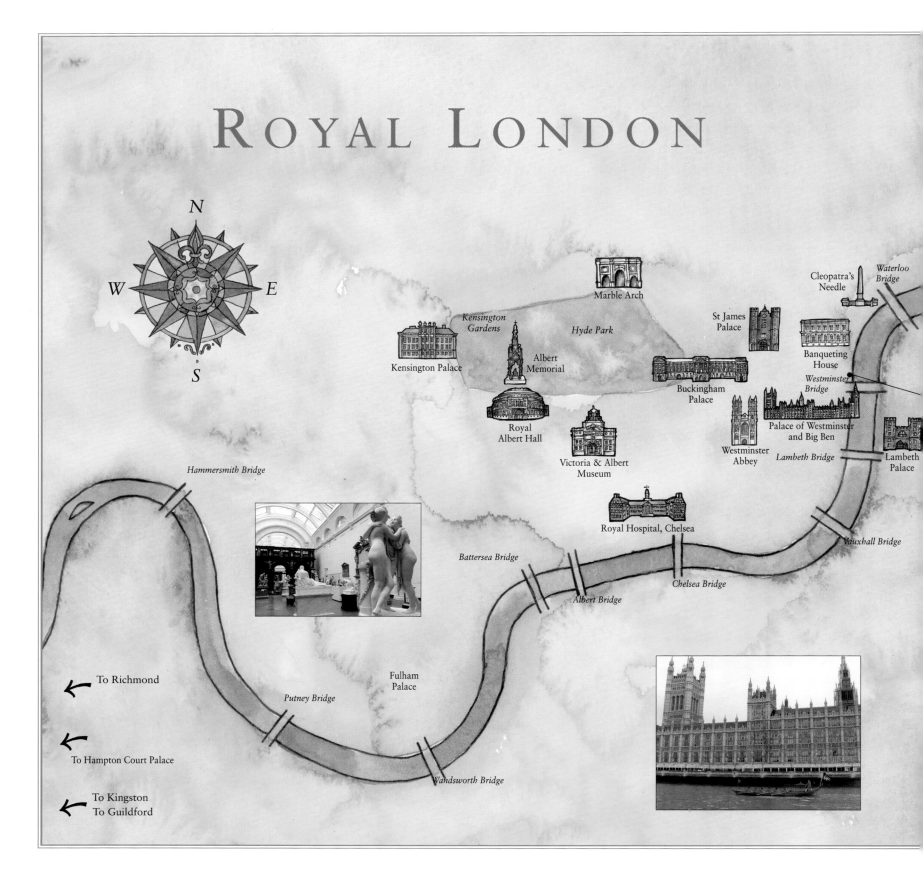

ROYAL LONDON

N

W   E

S

Marble Arch

Cleopatra's
Needle

Waterloo
Bridge

Kensington
Gardens

Hyde Park

St James
Palace

Albert
Memorial

Banqueting
House

Kensington Palace

Buckingham
Palace

Westminster
Bridge

Royal
Albert Hall

Palace of Westminster
and Big Ben

Westminster
Abbey

Lambeth
Palace

Victoria & Albert
Museum

Lambeth Bridge

Hammersmith Bridge

Royal Hospital, Chelsea

Vauxhall Bridge

Battersea Bridge

Chelsea Bridge

Albert Bridge

Fulham
Palace

To Richmond

Putney Bridge

To Hampton Court Palace

Wandsworth Bridge

To Kingston
To Guildford

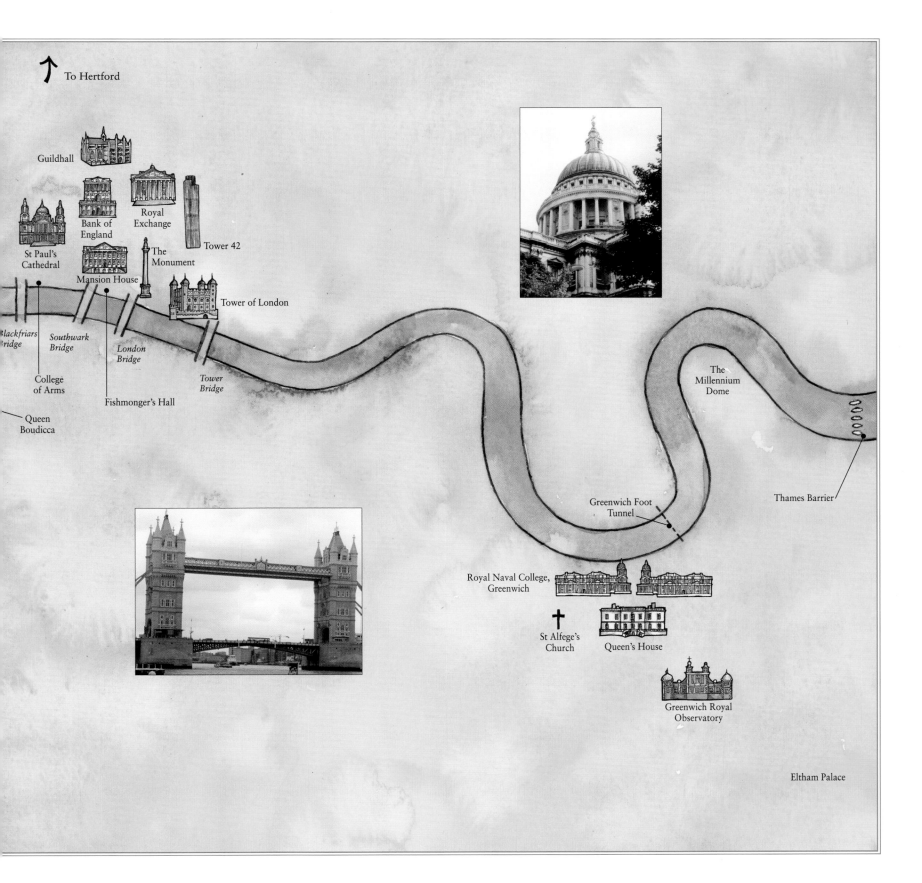

Guildhall

Bank of
England

Royal
Exchange

Tower 42

St Paul's
Cathedral

Mansion House

The
Monument

Tower of London

Blackfriars
Bridge

Southwark
Bridge

London
Bridge

Tower
Bridge

College
of Arms

Fishmonger's Hall

Queen
Boudicca

The
Millennium
Dome

Thames Barrier

Greenwich Foot
Tunnel

Royal Naval College,
Greenwich

St Alfege's
Church

Queen's House

Greenwich Royal
Observatory

Eltham Palace

SAXONS

NORMANS

Dates after name of sovereign denote length of his/her reign.

	EDWARD THE CONFESSOR 1042–66 d. 1066	HAROLD II Jan 1066– Oct 1066 d. 1066	WILLIAM I (THE CONQUEROR) 1066–87 d. 1087	WILLIAM II 1087–1100 d. 1100

ST PAUL'S CATHEDRAL

- 604 St Paul's Cathedral founded by St Ethelbert, the first Christian king in England.
- 610 St Paul's Cathedral completed (the first of five buildings on the site).

- 1087 St Paul's Cathedral destroyed by fire; rebuilt by Maurice, Bishop of London.

- 1087 Approves rebuilding of St Paul's Cathedral, a much larger church which becomes known as Old St Paul's. No further major work until 1634.

WESTMINSTER ABBEY & PALACE

- 730–40 Offa, king of Mercia, founds Westminster Abbey (the Monastery of St Peter on Thorney Island); later sacked by the Danes and abandoned.

- c. 1050–65 Moves from Wardrobe Palace near St Paul's to restore Westminster; builds a residence and rebuilds Westminster Abbey in the Norman (or Romanesque) style; portions of Edward's abbey survive in the Chapel of the Pyx (forms undercroft of the former monks' dormitory), named for the Pyx, a box with the standard pieces of gold and silver currency against which current coinage was checked annually for weight and metal.
- 1065, 28 Dec Westminster Abbey consecrated; Edward's remains were interred behind the High Altar after his death.

- 1066, 25 Dec William crowned in Westminster Abbey; all sovereigns (except Edward V and Edward VIII) have been crowned here since 1066.

- Crowned in Westminster Abbey.
- 1097–9 Palace of Westminster rebuilt; construction of Westminster Hall (the largest Norman hall in England).

TOWER OF LONDON

- 1066 Norman forces build a simple palisaded enclosure – on the site of what was to be the White Tower, nucleus of the Tower of London – at the southeast angle of London's Roman wall.

- 1097 White Tower completed.

ST ALBANS CATHEDRAL

- 1077–88 Construction of original Norman church at St Albans by Paul de Caen.

- *Rebuilds Waltham Abbey (founded 1030, later extended under Henry II); Harold was buried here after the Battle of Hastings.*

SAXON AND VIKING KINGS

ALFRED *(871–99) d. 899*
- *886 London recaptured from the Vikings; Alfred builds a citadel built to protect the town.*

EDWARD THE ELDER *(899–924) d. 924*
Crowned at Kingston-upon-Thames, 900.

ATHELSTAN *(924–39) d. 939*
Crowned at Kingston-upon-Thames.

EDMUND THE MAGNIFICENT *(939–46) d. 946*
Crowned at Kingston-upon-Thames.

EADRED *(946–55) d. 955*
Crowned at Kingston-upon-Thames.

EADWIG THE FAIR *(955–59) d. 959*
Crowned at Kingston-upon-Thames, 956.

EDGAR *(959–75) d. 975*
Crowned at Bath, 973.
- *961 St Paul's Cathedral destroyed by fire.*

EDWARD THE MARTYR *(975–8) d. 978*
Crowned at Kingston-upon-Thames.

AETHELRED THE UNREADY *(978–1016) d. 1016*
Crowned at Kingston-upon-Thames.

EDMUND IRONSIDE *(Apr 1016–Nov 1016) d. 1016*

CNUT (CANUTE) *((1016–35) d. 1035*

HAROLD HAREFOOT *(1035/6–40) d. 1040*

HARTHACANUT *(1040–2) d. 1042*

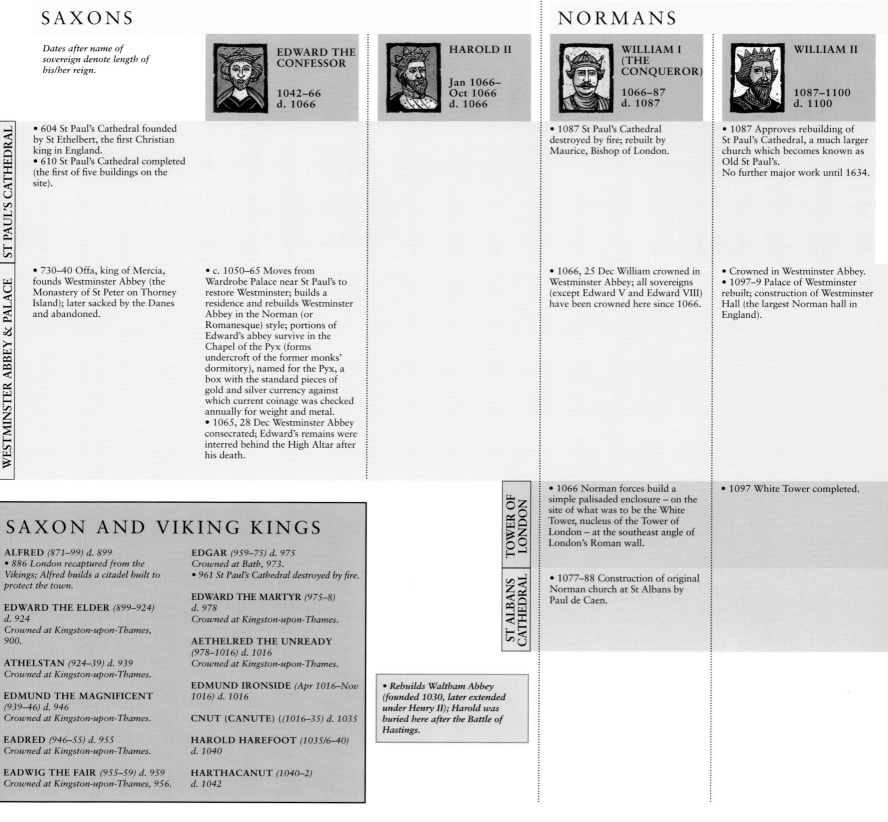

ANGEVINS

HENRY I	STEPHEN	HENRY II	RICHARD I	JOHN
1100–35 d. 1135	1135–54 d. 1154	1154–89 d. 1189	1189–99 d. 1199	1199–1216 d. 1216

• 1176–1209 First stone bridge built over the Thames by Peter of Colechurch.

HENRY I	STEPHEN	HENRY II	RICHARD I	JOHN
• Crowned in Westminster Abbey. • 1110–50 Completion of the nave of Westminster Abbey.	• Crowned in Westminster Abbey. • Royal Chapel of St Stephen built at Westminster.	• Crowned in Westminster Abbey. • 1163, 13 Oct The body of Edward the Confessor (canonised 1161) is transferred to a shrine built by Henry in Westminster Abbey.	• Crowned in Westminster Abbey.	• Crowned in Westminster Abbey.

• 1148 Hospital of St Katherine established in Wapping by Queen Matilda (later refounded by Eleanor of Castile), and under the protection of the Queen ever since; hospital escaped dissolution during the Reformation; its church and grace-and-favour homes were removed to Regent's Park after the construction of St Katherine's Dock (1800); church re-established in Wapping after the Second World War.

• 1100 Chapel of St Peter ad Vincula built outside the palisade surrounding the Tower of London.

• Strengthening of the defences and enlargement of royal apartments at the Tower of London, including a Great Hall, and the King's and Queen's great chambers, in the inner bailey.

• William Longchamp enlarges moat and adds an outer bailey of new walls and towers to the Tower of London.

• 1195–1214 Nave of St Albans Cathedral lengthened; work suspended in 1197.

• Grants the City of London the right to collect its own taxes and choose its sheriffs.
• Queen Matilda orders the construction of Bow Bridge over the River Lea.

PLANTAGENETS

	HENRY III 1216–72 d. 1272	EDWARD I 1272–1307 d. 1307	EDWARD II 1307–27 deposed 1327 d. Sept 1327
WESTMINSTER ABBEY & PALACE	• Crowned in Westminster Abbey. • 1220 Lady Chapel added at east end of Westminster Abbey (demolished 16thC; now occupied by Henry VII's Chapel). • 1230s Additional apartments built at Westminster; the Great Chamber rebuilt as the Painted Chamber, with the addition of famous biblical murals. • 1241 Henry commissions a shrine to Edward the Confessor at Westminster Abbey. • From 1245 Rebuilding of Westminster Abbey by King's mason Henry de Reyns, and later by John of Gloucester (1253–4) and Robert of Beverly (1260–1); Norman church gradually demolished; foundation stone laid 6 July, 1245; work stops 1269. • c. 1250 First of four cloisters built at Westminster Abbey. • c. 1250 Construction of Chapter House at Westminster Abbey completed; King's Great Council met here in 1257, and then from the time of Edward I to Henry VIII. Parliament met in the Chapter House during the 14thC (restored in the 19thC by Sir George Gilbert Scott). • c. 1255 Chancel, transepts, crossing and first bay of nave completed at Westminster Abbey; nave extended by four more bays during 1260s. • 1269, 13 Oct The body of St Edward the Confessor is transferred to a new shrine in still-unfinished Westminster Abbey; work on the nave stops until 1375.	• Crowned in Westminster Abbey. • 1290 Death of Edward's wife, Eleanor of Castile; crosses erected at every town where her body rested on the way to Westminster; the 12th was Waltham Cross, the 13th and last was at Charing Cross (site now marked by a stone spire, designed by E. M. Barry and carved by T. Earp, in the forecourt of Charing Cross Station). • 1292 Rebuilding begins of St Stephen's Chapel at Palace of Westminster (early 14thC crypt chapel survives); the Great Gateway northwest of Westminster Hall was also rebuilt. • 1296 Stone of Scone, captured from the Scots, placed in Westminster Abbey (returned to Scotland 1996). • 1298 Fire damages Westminster Abbey.	• Crowned in Westminster Abbey.
TOWER OF LONDON	• From 1220, Tower of London extensively rebuilt and enlarged through the construction of inner curtain wall and towers (Wakefield, Coldharbour and former Lanthorn Towers), and start of outer curtain wall along the Thames (from Lanthorn Tower to Bell Tower). Henry also rebuilds the Great Hall (completed 1234; demolished) and rebuilds the Chapel of St Peter ad Vincula. • From 1238 work begins to extend the Tower of London to the north, east and northwest, and to provide a towered curtain wall and moat. • 1241 Henry commissions refurbishment of Chapel of St Peter ad Vincula (at that time housing two chapels).	• 1275–85 Construction of moat and curtain walls completed at Tower of London; completion of western part of inner curtain wall, raising of Beauchamp Tower, construction of southern outer ward (including St Thomas's Tower and main water gate), gate towers of new main land entrance (Lion Tower, Middle Tower and Byward Tower); construction of Tower Wharf begins. • 1285–9 Rebuilding of Chapel of St Peter ad Vincula, Tower of London. • 1300 Royal Mint established in the Tower of London.	• Portions of southern outer curtain wall (from St Thomas's Tower to St Katharine's Tower) of Tower of London raised and strengthened.
ST ALBANS CATHEDRAL	• 1230 Completion of west front of St Albans Cathedral.		• 1323 Partial collapse and rebuilding of St Albans Cathedral. No further major building work until 1403.
WHITEHALL PALACE	• c. 1240 Archbishop of York builds York Place in Westminster – later the site of the Palace of Whitehall – as the London residence of the archbishops of York.		
ELTHAM PALACE		• 1295 Eltham Palace built by Anthony Bek, Bishop of Durham. • 1305 Bishop Bek presents Eltham Palace to Edward of Carnarvon (future Edward II).	• 1311 Eltham Palace acquired by the Queen.

• *1306 Edward's second wife, Margaret, begins rebuilding the church of the Grey or Franciscan Friars near Newgate, where the heart of Queen Eleanor was buried.*

LANCASTER

EDWARD III 1327–77 d. 1377	RICHARD II 1377–99 deposed 1399 d. 1400	HENRY IV 1399–1413 d. 1413	HENRY V 1413–22 d. 1422	HENRY VI 1422–71 deposed 1461 restored 1470 deposed 1471 d. 1471
• Crowned in Westminster Abbey. • 1347 Rebuilding of St Stephen's Chapel completed at Westminster (secularised during the Reformation; became meeting place of Parliament). • 1365–6 Jewel Tower built at Westminster, probably by Henry Yvele; served as Edward's personal treasury; from 1661–1864, the Tower housed the Lords' record office (now a museum). • 1352–66 Completion of Westminster Abbey cloisters. • 1375 Demolition of the remainder of Norman nave of Westminster Abbey; work on the new nave resumes; work on west front continues until c. 1500; the new nave was built by master mason Henry Yvele, under the direction of Abbot Nicholas Litlyngton (1362–86). • Jerusalem Chamber (in Abbot's house) built under Abbot Litlyngton; entered from Jericho Parlour, built under Abbot John Islip (1500–32).	• Crowned in Westminster Abbey. • 1390–1400 Nave of Westminster Abbey completed. • 1393 Richard orders rebuilding of Westminster Hall; carried out by master mason Henry Yvele; Hugh Herland makes new hammerbeam timber roof (1394–1402).	• Crowned in Westminster Abbey.	• Crowned in Westminster Abbey. • 1422–c. 1430 Construction of Henry V's Chantry Chapel in Westminster Abbey.	• Crowned in Westminster Abbey.
• From 1336 Remainder of southern outer curtain wall of Tower of London heightened and strengthened (from Byward Tower to St Thomas's Tower); Tower Wharf extended (1338–9); south inner curtain wall heightened and strengthened from Bell Tower to Salt Tower (1339); new gateway constructed between Lanthorn and Salt Towers (1341). • 1348–55 New watergate of the Cradle Tower built at Tower of London. • 1365–70 Tower Wharf rebuilt in stone.				

RICHMOND PALACE

EDWARD III	RICHARD II	HENRY IV	HENRY V	HENRY VI
• 1377 Edward dies at Shene, a manor house used occasionally by the monarch, and extended during his reign (later the site of Richmond Palace).	• 1394 Richard orders manor house at Shene to be demolished.			

EDWARD III	RICHARD II	HENRY IV	HENRY V	HENRY VI
• 1350s Development of apartments and gardens at Eltham Palace; became a favoured royal residence throughout 14thC and 15thC.		• 1399–1407 Renovation of Eltham Palace; additional storey built.		

ST ALBANS CATHEDRAL — **GREENWICH PALACE**

EDWARD III	RICHARD II	HENRY IV	HENRY V	HENRY VI
		• 1403–12 Thomas Wolvey builds Curfew (Clock) Tower. No further major building work until 1877.		• Humphrey, Duke of Gloucester (Regent to the infant King) acquires the freehold to the manor of Greenwich; builds a house called Bella Court (c. 1426), which later (1445) passes to Margaret of Anjou, wife of Henry VI; Margaret enlarges it and renames it Placentia (or Plaisaunce) – later a favourite royal residence.

	YORK			TUDOR	
	 EDWARD IV 1461–83 deposed 1470 restored 1471 d. 1483	 EDWARD V April 1483–June 1483; deposed 1483; d. alleg. murdered summer 1483	 RICHARD III 1483–85 d. 1485	 HENRY VII 1485–1509 d. 1509	 HENRY VIII 1509–47 d. 1547
WESTMINSTER ABBEY & PALACE	• Crowned in Westminster Abbey.		• Crowned in Westminster Abbey.	• Crowned in Westminster Abbey. • 1503 Henry begins new Lady Chapel at Westminster Abbey to house the remains of Henry VI (original 13thC Lady Chapel pulled down); probably designed by Robert Vertue and his brother, William.	• Crowned in Westminster Abbey. • 1512 Henry VII's Lady Chapel at Westminster Abbey completed; Henry VII and his consort Elizabeth of York buried behind the altar (tomb made by Pietro Torrigiano, 1512–18); chapel also contains tombs of Elizabeth I, Mary Tudor. Tomb of Mary, Queen of Scots (erected by James I) located beside that of Henry VII.
TOWER OF LONDON		• 1483 Edward allegedly murdered in the Tower of London.		• 1506 Building of King's Gallery at the Tower of London (runs from Lanthorn Tower to Salt Tower).	• Acquires more than 60 residences – including 13 in and around London – during his reign; the last sovereign to use the Tower of London as chief residence. • Corner bastions of Tower of London – Legge's Mount and Brass Mount – added during Henry's reign; Brick Tower built c. 1510–20 as a residence for the Master of the Ordnance.
RICHMOND PALACE				• 1501 Richmond Palace is built on the site of the burned Shene manor house; a favoured residence under the Tudors, but falls into decline under the Stuarts and the Commonwealth. • 1506 Richmond Palace damaged by fire.	HAMPTON COURT • 1514 Cardinal Wolsey leases manor of Hampton Court from the Knights of St John, and builds a lavish palace beside the Thames: the West Front, Base Court, Clock Court, Chapel and Master Carpenter's Court date from this time. The master mason was probably Henry Redman. At that time Wolsey also took over York Place (later the Palace of Whitehall) as his town residence, enlarging and adding to it. • 1529 Cardinal Wolsey offers Hampton Court to the King. • 1530 Palaces of Hampton Court and York Place seized from Cardinal Wolsey. York Place becomes Henry's main London residence. At Hampton Court
WHITEHALL PALACE					• 1529–32 Henry appropriates what becomes Whitehall as royal palace. Henry builds two gatehouses in what is now Whitehall: the Holbein Gate and the King Street Gate. Palace of Whitehall grew in stages from this period: among Henry's additions were a tiltyard, cockpit, bowling alley and tennis court.
ELTHAM PALACE	• 1475–9 Extensions to Eltham Palace, including the Great Hall.				• 1520s New chapel built at Eltham Palace, but palace is neglected from this time. No further major work to the original palace after this time.
GREENWICH PALACE				• Henry's favourite residence was Placentia, in Greenwich; he refaced it with bricks and called it Greenwich Palace.	• 1536 Greenwich Palace becomes a favourite royal residence; Henry adds an armoury and tiltyard with adjoining watch towers, and lays out extensive gardens.
HATFIELD PALACE	• 1480–90 Construction of the palace at Hatfield by the Bishop of Ely (becomes Crown property after the dissolution of the monasteries, 1534–9).				• 1538 Hatfield Palace is acquired by Henry in exchange for monastic lands in East Anglia; Hatfield becomes a nursery for the King's children.

• As Duke of Gloucester (and protector to the infant Edward V), Richard lives at Crosby Place in Bishopsgate (built 1466); the hall was removed and re-erected in Chelsea in 1926.

	 **EDWARD VI** 1547–53 d. 1553	**MARY I** 1553–58 d. 1558	 **ELIZABETH I** 1558–1603 d. 1603
• 1512 Fire damages the Palace of Westminster; ceases to be a royal residence. • 1540 Monastery of Westminster Abbey dissolved.	• Crowned in Westminster Abbey.	• Crowned in Westminster Abbey. • 1553 Garden of the Convent, a produce garden for Westminster Abbey, sold by the Crown to Sir John Russell (redeveloped in 17thC as Covent Garden). • 1557 Partial restoration of the shrine of St Edward the Confessor in Westminster Abbey; shrine had been dismantled and the coffin stored during the Reformation; stone base reassembled and coffin placed in upper part.	• Crowned in Westminster Abbey. • 1560 Westminster Abbey re-founded as a Collegiate Royal, a Royal Peculiar under a Dean and Chapter but subject only to the sovereign.
• 1512 Fire destroys Chapel of St Peter ad Vincula (Tower of London); rebuilt c. 1519–20. • 1530s Jewel House built next to the White Tower (later demolished). • 1532–3 General repairs to walls of Tower of London, and refurbishment of royal lodgings in the southeast quarter (these buildings demolished in 17thC); Henry ceases to use the Tower as a residence (from c. 1540, the Tower is used mainly as an armoury and prison). No further major work undertaken until 1843.			
new wings are added to the west front; Great Hall and a new court built (later to contain Wren's fountain); remodelling of Clock Court; buildings added to the north and east of the chapel. Master mason was John Molton, with interiors by John Nedeham. The Tennis Court was also built at around this time. • Manor of Oatlands in Surrey acquired to add its lands to Hampton Court. • 1535–6 Alterations to the Chapel at Hampton Court. • 1536 Completion of the Great Hall at Hampton Court. • 1536 King's New Stable built at Hampton Court. • 1540 Nicholas Oursian builds the astronomical clock at Hampton Court.			• 1570 Queen's New Stable built at Hampton Court.
			• 1581–2 Timber and canvas Banqueting House built at Whitehall, designed by Thomas Graves.
ST JAMES'S PALACE • 1531 Henry purchases 180 acres south and west of Charing Cross from Eton College; construction of St James's Palace (1532–40) on the site of the Hospital of St James.			
• 1513 Royal dockyards established at Deptford and Woolwich. • 1534–9 Dissolution of the monasteries; greatest shift in land ownership in English history; extensive lands become Crown property. • The Temple, previously owned by the Knights of St John, becomes the site of Henry's Bridewell Palace. • 1536 Hyde Park becomes Crown land when Henry appropriates 620 acres of farmland from Westminster Abbey; land is enclosed and becomes royal hunting grounds (western portion is now Kensington Palace Gardens). • 1538 Henry commissions Nonsuch Palace in Surrey, 10 miles south of the Thames (between Epsom and Ewell), close to a 1,700-acre deer park; built with stone taken from dissolved Merton Priory. • 1539 Marylebone Park acquired for use as a hunting forest; sold at auction after the Civil War, re-acquired by the Crown at the Restoration.	• 1547–52 Somerset House built in the classical style by Edward Seymour, Duke of Somerset, Protector of the infant King; later the residence of Elizabeth I, and the Stuart queens.	• Nonsuch Palace given to the Earl of Arundel in exchange for lands in Suffolk (returned to Charles I's widow after the Restoration).	• Vacates many of Henry's palaces, partly for financial reasons; Greenwich and Whitehall become the main royal residences. • 1581 Hunting pavilion at Chingford (built by Henry VIII) converted into a lodge. • 1591 Nonsuch Palace bought back from the Earl of Arundel.

STUARTS

	JAMES I — 1603–35, d. 1625	CHARLES I — 1625–49, beheaded Jan 1649	CHARLES II — 1660–85, d. 1685
ST PAUL'S CATHEDRAL		• 1634 Inigo Jones appointed as surveyor to the commission charged with restoring St Paul's Cathedral: refaces west, north and south walls of the nave and the walls of the transept; a giant portico, the gift of Charles I, is placed in front of west façade.	• 1666 Great Fire of London destroys much of the City; a week later Christopher Wren submits a rebuilding plan to the King. Royal proclamation announces the City will be rebuilt in brick and stone. • 1672 Charles II approves Wren's design for the rebuilding of St Paul's Cathedral. Wren revises his design in 1673.
WESTMINSTER ABBEY & PALACE	• Crowned in Westminster Abbey.	• Crowned in Westminster Abbey. • 1649 Trial of Charles I held in Westminster Hall; the King spent his last night in St James's Palace, and was beheaded outside the Banqueting House on 30 Jan, 1649.	• Crowned in Westminster Abbey.
HAMPTON COURT			• Improvements made to the gardens at Hampton Court, including diversion of the River Colne to supply water for fountains.
WHITEHALL PALACE	• Whitehall is James's main London residence; his queen, Anne of Denmark, operates her own household at Somerset House (known as Denmark House). • 1607 New Banqueting Hall built at Whitehall (destroyed by fire in 1619). • 1617–20 Inigo Jones builds an addition to Whitehall to house James's favourite, the Marquis of Buckingham. • 1619 James and Inigo Jones plan rebuilding of the Palace; only the Banqueting House was built (1619–25).	• 1626–7 Inigo Jones builds a Clock House at Whitehall and a new gallery with an outside staircase leading into St James's Palace. • 1630 Inigo Jones and John Webb plan the rebuilding of the Palace of Whitehall. • 1634 Peter Paul Rubens completes the ceiling of the Banqueting House, a painting depicting the apotheosis of King James.	*• 1661 The New Gallery (designed by Inigo Jones) built at Somerset House for Henrietta Maria, the Queen Mother, during extensive restoration work.* *• 1669 Queen Catherine of Braganza acquires Somerset House upon the death of Henrietta Maria; Catherine is asked to leave in 1688.* *• 1670 Nonsuch Palace given to the King's mistress, Lady Castlemaine.* *• 1671 Construction of Temple Bar, a large gateway built of Portland stone, in Chancery Lane, allegedly designed by Christopher Wren. Marks the boundary of the City of London and the City of Westminster.* *• 1671–7 Construction of The Monument by Christopher Wren and Robert Hooke, near the site of the outbreak of the Great Fire; relief carvings feature Charles II.*
GREENWICH PALACE	• 1613 Palace of Greenwich settled on Anne of Denmark. • 1616 Inigo Jones begins construction of Queen's House at Greenwich (next to the Palace of Greenwich); work stops soon after; the Queen dies in 1619.	• 1629–35 Completion of Queen's House at Greenwich.	• Greenwich Park laid out. • 1662 John Webb extends Queen's House at Greenwich. • 1662–9 John Webb designs and begins construction of a new palace at Greenwich; the old Tudor palace is pulled down; only the west range of the new palace was built, which survives as the eastern parts of the King Charles Block of the Royal Naval Hospital.
HATFIELD PALACE	• 1607 James suggests to Robert Cecil that he exchange the palace at Hatfield for Cecil's house, Theobalds; Theobalds becomes James's favourite residence; sold during the Commonwealth and later ruined. • 1608–12 Hatfield Palace pulled down and new house built by Robert Cecil.		
ST JAMES'S PALACE	• 1609–10 Library installed at St James's Palace, possibly by Inigo Jones.	• 1623–7 Queen's Chapel built by Inigo Jones next to St James's Palace (in 1809, the building of Marlborough Road separated the palace from the chapel).	• 1661 Charles makes limited improvements to St James's Palace. Christopher Wren commissioned to add state apartments; St James's Palace assigned to the Duke of York as his residence. • 1662 King's gardener, John Rose, commissioned to redesign St James's Park. The park is opened to the public for the first time. Green Park laid out.
BUCKINGHAM PALACE	• 1609 James establishes a mulberry garden, on the site of Buckingham Palace, to produce silk; plants 30,000 mulberry trees; the site of his aviary is now Birdcage Walk.	*• 1631 Dutch House (later Kew Palace) built at Kew by Samuel Fortrey.* *• 1635 Henrietta Maria commissions a Roman Catholic chapel for Somerset House.* *• 1647 Charing Cross demolished.*	• 1662–9 Charles lays out a pell mell ground on what is now The Mall. • 1674 Goring House, built on the site of James I's mulberry garden, destroyed by fire; replaced by Arlington House and later by Buckingham House.
ROYAL HOSPITAL, CHELSEA			• 1682 Foundation stone laid for Royal Hospital, Chelsea on the site of a theological college established by James I; Royal Hospital designed and built by Christopher Wren, includes a statue of Charles II by Grinling Gibbons.

20

	JAMES II 1685–88 declared to have abdicated Dec 1688 d. 1701	WILLIAM III AND 1688–1702 d. 1702	MARY II 1688–94 d. 1694
• 1675 Wren's new design for St Paul's Cathedral, featuring a dome and spire, receives the Royal Warrant – thereafter known as the Warrant Design. • 1675, 21 June Foundation stone laid for St Paul's Cathedral.		• 1695 Chancel of St Paul's Cathedral consecrated. No further major building work.	
	• Crowned in Westminster Abbey.	• Crowned in Westminster Abbey. • 1698–1723 Restoration of the exterior of Westminster Abbey by Wren.	
		• From 1689, Christopher Wren rebuilds Hampton Court as principal royal residence; one of Henry VIII's courtyards replaced by Fountain Court, around which state rooms (Tudor state rooms demolished), East Front, south range of Clock Court, and Orangery built.	• William lays out the gardens and park to the east of Hampton Court, including a mile-long straight canal. • 1694 Death of Queen Mary; work stops until 1698. • 1700 Completion of the Banqueting House at Hampton Court by Wren.
	• 1685–8 Christopher Wren rebuilds a section facing the Privy Garden, and builds a range (with a chapel) for James's queen. • 1686 Bronze statue of James II made by Grinling Gibbons for Whitehall; later moved to St James's Park, and now stands outside the National Gallery.	• 1698, January Palace of Whitehall almost totally destroyed by fire (except the Banqueting House and the Whitehall Gate).	• 1698 Wren transforms the Banqueting House, Whitehall, into a chapel; serves as Chapel Royal until 1890.
• 1664 Foundation stone laid for the new palace at Greenwich. • 1675–6 Construction of original buildings of Royal Observatory in Greenwich Park, probably by Christopher Wren.		• 1694 When William and Mary decide not to live at Greenwich, Christopher Wren is commissioned to build a naval hospital, on the site of the new palace commissioned by Charles II; King William Building begun 1698, Queen Mary Building begun 1699.	• 1696 Work begins on Royal Naval Hospital, Greenwich. • 1700–3 Queen Anne Block of Royal Naval Hospital built by Nicholas Hawksmoor.
	• *c. 1687 Demolition of Nonsuch Palace.*		
		• 1689 Royal Hospital, Chelsea: central lantern completed. • 1692 Opening of the Royal Hospital, Chelsea.	
	KENSINGTON PALACE	• 1689 To escape the smoke of Westminster, William buys Nottingham House from the Earl of Nottingham; renamed Kensington Palace, it becomes the chief royal residence in London until the death of George II. • 1689–90 Kensington Palace extended and improved by Christopher Wren and his assistant, Nicholas Hawksmoor.	

STUARTS

HANOVER

ANNE

1702–14
d. 1714

GEORGE I

1714–27
d. 1727

GEORGE II

1727–60
d. 1760

WESTMINSTER ABBEY & PALACE

• Crowned in Westminster Abbey.

• Crowned in Westminster Abbey.
• 1725 Henry VII's Chapel at Westminster Abbey designated the Chapel of the Order of the Bath.

• Crowned in Westminster Abbey.
• 1735–45 West towers of Westminster Abbey completed by John James (to designs by Nicholas Hawksmoor).

HAMPTON COURT

• Chapel at Hampton Court redecorated by Sir Christopher Wren and Grinling Gibbons.

• Completion of the decoration of the state rooms at Hampton Court.
• 1732 North front of Hampton Court Palace heightened; entrance built from Clock to Fountain Court.

WHITEHALL PALACE

• 1723 Removal of the King Street Gate from Whitehall.

• 1759 Demolition of the Holbein Gate, Whitehall.

GREENWICH PALACE

• *1716 Establishment of the Royal Arsenal, Woolwich.*
• *1722 Prince of Wales (the future George II) takes up residence at Richmond Lodge in Old Deer Park (Richmond Palace had been demolished after the execution of Charles I).*
• *1725 Marble Hill House built at Twickenham for George's mistress, the Countess of Suffolk (later occupied by George IV's secret wife, Mrs Fitzherbert).*

• *1732 Carlton House purchased by Frederick, Prince of Wales, as a ceremonial home; alterations to the house carried out by William Kent.*
• *1741 Foundation of Royal Military Academy at Woolwich.*
• *1751 Death of Frederick, Prince of Wales; his widow, Augusta, commissions further alterations to Carlton House.*
• *1758 Carlton House granted to George, Prince of Wales.*
• *1759 Princess Augusta dedicates nine acres of land at Kew for botanical study – foundation of Kew Gardens.*

St JAMES'S PALACE

• 1702 Court is established at St James's Palace; the palace has been the sovereign's official residence ever since.

• 1716–17 Nicholas Hawksmoor adds a brick arcade to the Stable Yard of St James's Palace.

BUCKINGHAM PALACE

KENSINGTON PALACE

• 1702 John Vanbrugh and Nicholas Hawksmoor design and build the Orangery at Kensington Palace; new rooms built behind the King's Gallery, formal French garden laid out, and 100 acres of Hyde Park enclosed as a deer paddock.

• 1714–21 Extensive rebuilding of Kensington Palace by William Benson: three new state rooms, probably designed by Colen Campbell; a self-contained residence built on the north side to house the King's mistress, the Duchess of Kendal; later passed to the Prince of Wales; now known as Prince of Wales Court.
• 1724 William Kent commissioned to make improvements to Kensington Palace; as well as new state rooms, Kent decorates the main staircase and the coffered vault of the Cupola Room – the principal state room.

• Kensington Palace Gardens redesigned; Broad Walk laid out, Round Pond created.
• 1730 Queen Caroline creates the Serpentine, Hyde Park, by damming the Westbourne River.

KEW

• 1728 Queen Caroline leases the Dutch House at Kew for use by the royal family; becomes known as Kew Palace.
• 1730–5 The White House built at Kew (near Richmond Lodge) for Frederick, Prince of Wales and Princess Augusta; the White House remains the country residence of George III and Queen Charlotte until 1801; a sundial in Kew Gardens marks the site of the White House.

GEORGE III

1760–1820
Regency declared 1811
d. 1820

- Crowned in Westminster Abbey.

- 1771–3 Rebuilding of the Great Gatehouse at Hampton Court; palace not used as a royal residence after accession of George III.

- *1783 Prince of Wales receives his own establishment at Carlton House; the house is altered and enlarged (1784-96) by Henry Holland. Additions include: a Corinthian portico; interior decorated in the Chinese style (1788–90), additional rooms (from 1794) built for Prince of Wales's wife, Caroline; and an Ionic screen fronting Pall Mall.*

- 1805 Queen's House, Greenwich, sold by Caroline, Princess of Wales; becomes a school for seamen's children.

- 1809 East and south wings of St James's Palace damaged by fire (restored by 1813).

- 1761–2 George purchases Buckingham House, and assigns it to the Queen. Sir William Chambers commissioned to remodel Buckingham House as a royal residence.
- 1762 The Queen takes up residence in Buckingham House.
- 1775 Buckingham House renamed The Queen's House.
- 1800 James Wyatt commissioned to build an imperial-style staircase for The Queen's House (Buckingham House).

- From 1760 Kensington Palace ceases to be main royal residence.

- 1788 King George and Queen Charlotte take up residence at Kew Palace.

THE REGENCY

- *1812 John Nash draws up plans for Regent Street and Regent's Park, to be laid out on the former Marylebone Park. The design was to include a villa for the Prince Regent (never built), with Regent Street and Portland Place planned as the route to the new park.*
- *1813 John Nash builds the Gothic Dining Room and the Corinthian Room at Carlton House.*
- *1816 Claremont (near Esher) acquired by the Crown; becomes the home of Charlotte, daughter of the Prince Regent, when she marries Leopold of Saxe-Coburg; house built from 1769 for Lord Clive by Capability Brown and Henry Holland. After 1848, Claremont becomes the home of the exiled French royal family.*
- *1817 Work begins on the Regent St/Regent's Park scheme.*
- *1817 Marlborough House passes to the Crown; assigned to Princess Charlotte and Leopold of Saxe-Coburg; after her death, Leopold stays in the house until 1831.*
- *From 1820, Royal Mews cleared to make way for construction of Trafalgar Square.*

- Early 19thC Kensington Palace re-opened as accommodation for Caroline of Brunswick.

GEORGE IV

1820–30
(Prince Regent from 1811)
d. 1830

- Crowned in Westminster Abbey.

- *1820 Lancaster House (originally York House) designed by Robert Smirke.*
- *1825–9 Godolphin House demolished; work begins on York House, for the Duke of York; though designed by Robert Smirke, it was built to new plans by Benjamin Wyatt. When the duke died, the house was acquired by the Marquess of Stafford (1st Duke of Sutherland); construction was completed under the 2nd duke. The house was later renamed Lancaster House and presented to the nation.*
- *1830 Trafalgar Square completed; later incorporates equestrian statue of Charles I by Le Sueur (1633) and an equestrian statue of George IV, originally made for Marble Arch (1829–43).*
- *1830s Smirke and Wyatt add a top storey to Lancaster House (to house servants' quarters).*
- *1827–32 Construction of Carlton House Terrace by John Nash on the site of Carlton House (Carlton House demolished 1829).*

- 1825 Clarence House (off Stable Yard, adjacent to St James's Palace) built by Nash for Duke of Clarence (the future William IV).

- 1824–5 New Royal Mews built near The Queen's House (Buckingham House), which becomes known as The King's House.
- 1826 Nash commissioned to transform The King's House into a royal palace, to be known as Buckingham Palace; Nash adds new state and semi-state rooms on Principal Floor and Ground Floor; reconstructs Entrance Hall and Grand Staircase; north and south wings demolished and rebuilt;

- Nash commissioned to redesign St James's Park; transforms Charles II's straight canal into an irregular lake.

Octagon Library converted into a chapel.
- 1828–32 Construction of the entrance gate to Buckingham Palace, incorporating a triumphal arch designed by John Flaxman – to commemorate the battles of Trafalgar and Waterloo. The arch was later re-erected on Oxford Street as Marble Arch. In 1831 Nash dismissed from Buckingham Palace project for extravagance; replaced by Edward Blore, who completes the work in 1837.

HANOVER

	WILLIAM IV 1830–37 d. 1837	VICTORIA 1837–1901 d. 1901	

WESTMINSTER ABBEY & PALACE

WILLIAM IV
- Crowned in Westminster Abbey.
- 1834, 16 October Last remnants of the Palace of Westminster destroyed by fire (except Westminster Hall, crypt of St Stephen's Chapel and part of the cloisters); William offers Buckingham Palace as a temporary home for Parliament but it is declined.

VICTORIA
- Crowned in Westminster Abbey.
- 1840 Rebuilding of Houses of Parliament begins; designed and built by Sir Charles Barry and Augustus Welby Pugin.
- 1847 New House of Lords opens at Westminster.
- 1852 Remainder of new Houses of Parliament opened; includes Royal Entrance, Queen's Robing Room, Royal Gallery and Prince's Chamber.

- 1858 Completion of Clock Tower at Westminster (Houses of Parliament) to house Big Ben.
- 1860 Statue of Richard I by Marochetti placed in Old Palace Yard, Westminster.
- 1860 Completion of Victoria Tower at Westminster (Houses of Parliament).
- 1866 Restoration of Chapter House by Sir George Gilbert Scott.

TOWER OF LONDON

- 1843 Draining of Tower of London moat.
- 1845 Foundation stone of Waterloo Barracks, Tower of London, laid by Duke of Wellington.
- 1876–7 Restoration of Chapel of St Peter ad Vincula, Tower of London.

- 1894, 30 June Tower Bridge opened by Prince of Wales (designed by Sir Horace Jones).

> - *1850 Statue of Boudicca by Thomas Thornycroft placed on Victoria Embankment.*
> - *1873 Albert Suspension Bridge built across the Thames between Chelsea and Battersea.*
> - *1878 Cleopatra's Needle (c. 1500 B.C.) placed on Victoria Embankment.*

HAMPTON COURT

- 1839 State apartments at Hampton Court opened to the public.
- 1878 Rebuilding of Great Gatehouse at Hampton Court.

BUCKINGHAM PALACE

WILLIAM IV
- 1832 Additions to Buckingham Palace: Blore builds the Sovereign's Private Entrance – a columned screen running northward (the Garden Gate), balanced to the south by a columned Guard House.

> - *1831–4 Duke of York's Column built at the southern end of Nash's route from Regent's Park to Carlton House Terrace.*
> - *1834 Royal menagerie moved from Tower of London to Regent's Park, to become the nucleus of London Zoo; initially, 20 acres were leased from the Crown, later extended to 36 acres.*

VICTORIA
- 1837 First sovereign to take up residence in Buckingham Palace.
- 1842–3 Blore builds private chapel at Buckingham Palace on the site of Nash's southeast pavilion.
- 1847 East Range of Buckingham Palace (designed by Edward Blore) built by Thomas Cubitt to provide additional accommodation; triumphal arch removed; attic floor added, decorated with marble friezes intended for Marble Arch. Cost of the new construction is financed by the sale of the Royal Pavilion in Brighton.

- 1850 Triumphal arch (originally the ceremonial gateway to Nash's Buckingham Palace) moved to Hyde Park, becoming Marble Arch.
- 1853–5 Ballroom block added to Buckingham House by Sir James Pennethorne.

KENSINGTON PALACE

- 1851 Great Exhibition opens in Hyde Park; exhibition developed by Prince Albert and Henry Cole. Crystal Palace built near southern boundary of the park; profits from the exhibition enable Prince Albert to purchase land south of Hyde Park – the site of the Royal Albert Hall, Imperial College, Royal College of Art, Science Museum, Geological Museum, Natural History Museum, Victoria & Albert Museum and other institutions.

- 1863–72 Construction of Albert Memorial in Hyde Park.
- 1899, 24 May Kensington Palace re-opens following restoration; the palace is opened to the public.

KEW

- 1898 To mark her Diamond Jubilee (1897), Victoria donates Queen Charlotte's Cottage (summer house built at Kew in the 1770s); still a 'Historic Royal Palace'.

ST ALBANS CATHEDRAL

- 1877 Sir George Gilbert Scott begins restoration work on St Albans Cathedral but dies in 1878.
- 1879 Lord Grimthorpe completes restoration.

SAXE-COBURG   WINDSOR

 EDWARD VII 1901–10 d. 1910	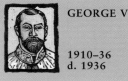 GEORGE V 1910–36 d. 1936	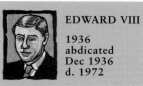 EDWARD VIII 1936 abdicated Dec 1936 d. 1972	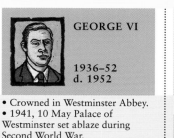 GEORGE VI 1936–52 d. 1952	ELIZABETH II 1952–
• Crowned in Westminster Abbey.	• Crowned in Westminster Abbey.		• Crowned in Westminster Abbey. • 1941, 10 May Palace of Westminster set ablaze during Second World War. • 1945 Sir Giles Gilbert Scott commissioned to rebuild Chamber of the House of Commons.	• Crowned in Westminster Abbey. *• 1959–60 Archaeological excavation of the site of Nonsuch Palace.* *• From 1964 Restoration of the Banqueting House to its original state.*
				• 1967 Jewel House built within Waterloo Barracks, Tower of London, to display the Crown Jewels (displays renovated mid-1990s).
	• 1924 Knot Garden laid out at Hampton Court, facing the Elizabethan corner of the south front.			• 1985 Fire damages one wing of Hampton Court Palace (restored from 1986).
• After Queen Victoria's death, Buckingham Palace is redecorated and electricity is installed. • 1901–13 Queen Victoria Memorial scheme: includes construction of the Mall (1910), Admiralty Arch (1911), Victoria Memorial (1911) designed by Sir Aston Webb, and addition of gates and railings to forecourt of Buckingham Palace (1911–14); North Centre Gate becomes the main entrance to the palace, with Central Gate used only for state occasions.	• 1913 East Front of Buckingham Palace refaced by Sir Aston Webb, using Portland stone to replace the soft Caen stone used in the 1840s. • 1919–25 Restoration of Nash's original work on Buckingham Palace.		• 1938 Conversion of Nash's northwest pavilion at Buckingham Palace into a swimming pool and squash court. • 1940 A bomb destroys the chapel at Buckingham Palace.	• 1961 Elizabeth plants an avenue of 34 Indian horse chestnut trees in the gardens at Buckingham Palace. • 1961–2 Rebuilding of the chapel at Buckingham Palace to house the Queen's Gallery and a smaller chapel. • 1993 State rooms at Buckingham Palace opened to the public (in summer) to raise money for restoration of Windsor Castle.
• 1909 Sunken Garden laid out at Kensington Palace.			• 1944 A flying bomb damages Kensington Palace.	• 1956 Renovation of the State Apartments at Kensington Palace. • 1972–5 Renovation work carried out on Kensington Palace (the palace housed the Museum of London from 1912–14 and 1951–76).
				• 1969 17th-century-style Queen's Garden opened by Elizabeth at Kew.

THE RIVER THAMES

London has grown up along the banks of the River Thames. The river has always been crucial to the city either

as a means of access, as a thriving port, for trade, or for business. Every aspect of the river's life has

been affected by or involved with the Crown, in countless different ways. As such, the River Thames is a vital

part of the story of the Crown and the capital.

While the Thames runs through the whole of modern London, there is one stretch that clearly illustrates

the role the river has played in the story, and that is between the Tower of London and the Royal Hospital at

Chelsea. This length of the Thames encompasses the very origins of London: the old harbour;

the main bridge; the original customs house; royal palaces; royal travel; great monuments

and forgotten treasures.

THE RIVER THAMES

A view downriver across the Pool of London.

THE TOWER OF LONDON

A Brief History

c. 1066
The original Tower of London was a wooden fort erected by William the Conqueror soon after the Battle of Hastings. It was built both for defence and as a symbol of power to subdue the defeated Saxon population.

Later, the wooden fort was replaced by a stone tower. This is thought to have been designed by Gundulf, a monk from the Abbey of Bec in Normandy, who became Bishop of Rochester. The keep was built in such a way that from every apartment the garrison could keep watch over the city and the surrounding countryside.

13th–19th century
The present White Tower is on the site of William the Conqueror's Norman keep. The curtain wall, towers and moat were added in the 13th century, along with a double drawbridge entrance.

The Tower has been a fortress and a royal palace for more than 900 years but is perhaps best known as a prison and place of execution, where prisoners of the Tower were guarded by Yeoman Warders. However, the Tower has also served as a royal armoury, royal mint, royal observatory and even a royal zoo.

In 1235, the Holy Roman Emperor gave Henry III three leopards, and the royal menagerie that developed was housed at the Tower. James I, the last monarch to live in the Tower, staged animal fights there. A polar bear once swam in the moat, but by 1822 the menagerie had dwindled to a grizzly bear, an elephant and some birds. Now, only six ravens remain; it is said that the White Tower, and the monarchy, will collapse if they leave. Ravens first took residence in the Tower just after the Great Fire of London but soon became a nuisance, with their droppings, feathers, and chicks. A petition was raised to Charles II to exterminate them but Charles, having heard the legend of the collapse of the monarchy if they left, decreed that six birds should always be kept in the Tower. Today they are looked after by the Raven Master.

20th century
The Tower's most important role has always been the security of the monarch, symbolised today by the safekeeping of the Crown Jewels there. Among the jewels displayed are twelve crowns, three Swords of Justice, the orb and Sceptre and the Sovereign's ring.

In the time of Henry VIII there were 13 royal palaces in and around London. Nine of them lay along the River Thames, from Windsor in the west to Greenwich in the east. Many no longer exist, and the most famous one, perhaps the Crown's most important building in the country, is not even thought of as a palace: the Tower of London. The Tower is better known as a prison, and as the home of the Crown Jewels.

THE POOL OF LONDON
The natural harbour of the Pool of London is the true heart of this vast and sprawling city which has been dominated for centuries by seafaring, trade and the Navy. The name London derives from the Celtic Llyn-Din, meaning 'the hill by the pool'.

The Pool forms the junction of the Thames as a port, with its docks and warehouses, and the river as the main thoroughfare through London. The Pool's importance stems from the fact that it is deep enough for large ships to anchor, after coming upriver on the tide, and has gravel ledges on the north and south shores, making it possible to bridge the river.

Tower Hill is all that remains today of 'the hill by the pool', half hidden by houses, but the strategic importance of both hill and pool is highlighted by the remaining presence of the Tower of London.

PRISONERS OF THE TOWER
Most prisoners were held in the Bloody Tower and looked after by the Yeoman Warders, but a few of higher rank were kept in the Queen's House under the direct supervision of the Governor.

State trials took place in Westminster Hall and prisoners would be ferried there and back along the river. Crowds would often gather along the banks to find out the verdict, in eager anticipation of a public execution.

When the boat returned to the Tower, the executioner would stand behind the accused and indicate the verdict with the head of his axe, pointing it towards the victim if guilty, away if innocent.

The majority of executions were public spectacles held on Tower Hill. Only a few were allowed the privilege of a private execution within the confines of the Tower itself.

RAVENS AT THE TOWER
Six ravens are kept at the Tower of London, as a safeguard against a prophecy that the monarchy will collapse if the ravens should ever leave the Tower.

THE TOWER OF LONDON

The Tower's first prisoner was also one of the few to escape. Ralf Flambard, Bishop of Durham,
was locked up in 1101 and managed to escape by lowering a rope from one of the windows
after he had got the guards drunk.

THE YEOMAN WARDERS

There are many theories as to why the Yeomen of the Guard and Yeoman Warders are commonly known as Beefeaters. One theory is that the Yeomen were allowed to eat the remains from the King's table, and another is that

they were allowed as much beef as they could fit on to the blade of a dagger. What we do know is that, until the 1800s, part of their salary was paid in beef.

The Yeomen of the Guard were formed in 1485 by Henry VII as a personal bodyguard to accompany the monarch at all times. In 1509, Henry VIII decided to leave 12 infirm Yeomen in the Tower to protect it. They became the Yeoman Warders, responsible for the security of the Tower and for state prisoners lodged there. When wearing state dress, Yeomen of the Guard can be distinguished from Yeoman Warders by the cross belt on which they used to carry an arquebus, a type of gun.

Today, the Yeomen of the Guard are selected from all the services except the Navy. There are about 40 of them, most of whom live with their families within the Tower. Sworn in as Special Constables, they have police powers within the precinct of the Tower, and are still responsible for its security. The Metropolitan Police may only enter the Tower with the permission of the Governor.

As the Queen's bodyguards, Yeomen of the Guard form part of the guard of honour at Westminster Abbey for coronations.

Yeoman Warders still perform the Ceremony of the Keys, which takes place every night at 9.53 pm: the chief Yeoman Warder marches towards the Byward Tower and calls for 'an escort for the keys'; four armed soldiers of the garrison march with him to the entrance gate beyond the Middle Tower, which is then locked; they march back and the gates of the Byward Tower are also locked; as they approach the Bloody Tower the sentry challenges them and a traditional exchange takes place:

> 'Halt, who goes there?'
> The chief Yeoman Warder replies, 'The Keys.'
> 'Whose Keys?'
> 'Queen Elizabeth's keys.'
> 'God preserve Queen Elizabeth!'
> The whole guard replies, 'Amen!'

YEOMAN WARDERS

A CLOSER LOOK

Traffic on Tower Bridge in 1910.

TOWER BRIDGE

Tower Bridge divides the Pool of London. Construction work on this magnificent gothic edifice began in 1885. For a long time the only bridge below London Bridge, it was designed by Horace Jones to be in architectural harmony with the Tower of London, and was opened with great ceremony on 30 June 1894.

The bascule bridge was a triumph of engineering. Its stone-clad steel frame supported the great weight of the lifting arms, and had lifts to the footbridge above. Huge steam engines powered the hydraulics responsible for raising and lowering the roadway to let larger ships pass through, and the walkway above allowed pedestrians to cross even when the bridge was in operation. The only time the steam engines failed was at the opening ceremony! It was electrified in 1976.

THE LONDON DOCKS

For centuries, London was primarily a tidal port – a long narrow city hugging the banks of the Thames. The river, and the trade which it attracted, were the main reasons for the city's importance and subsequent growth. Commercial docks were eventually built on the north shore of the river, including the West India Docks and the London Docks at Wapping, which now form part of the Docklands Development.

THE RIVER POLICE

By the 18th century, trade on the river was in chaos. The Legal Quays could not cope with the quantity of goods to be landed, warehousing was inadequate, and most loading and unloading took place on the open river, leading to ever-growing congestion and criminal activity. Twenty-one Sufferance Docks were built, but these eased the situation only slightly.

In the 1780s, London was one of the largest ports in the world, yet ships often waited a week before they could enter the port, and sometimes over a year before they could be unloaded. At one time, 1,770 ships were trying to moor, four or five deep, on buoys and moorings designed for 545. The line of ships often reached for two miles above London Bridge and four miles below, while more than 3,000 lighters and wherries continuously ferried cargo and people to and from the congested wharfs.

Gangs of pirates would strip ships, anchors and all; 'scuffle-hunters' would filch unguarded wares from the quayside; and 'mud-larks' would collect goods from the water's edge which had been thrown

overboard by accomplices. Total losses from this plunder were approaching £500,000 a year.

In 1798, the Marine Police Force was founded in an attempt to improve the situation. The idea was first mooted by Patrick Colquhoun and John Harriott after an approach from the West India Company. In July 1798, the first patrol set out from their base at Wapping High Street, close to Execution Dock.

The River Police were one of the first uniformed police forces in the world, preceding the Peelers (land police) by 31 years. The government paid for 200 armed watermen under a chief constable to patrol the river; the West India Company supplied and paid for watermen on the quays. The River Police patrolled in open rowing galleys and hired part-time ships' guards to oversee loading and unloading. It cost £4,200 to establish and equip the force, but within six months they had saved more than 25 times that amount. They were so effective that the criminal fraternity organised a riot which resulted in a policeman being killed on duty for the first time. Nevertheless, it was not until enclosed docks were built in the 19th century

that crime was really brought under control.

An Act of Parliament in 1800 officially recognised the Marine Police, and by the time the Metropolitan Police Force was formed in 1829, they had stations at Wapping, Waterloo and Blackwall. Six-hour patrols were mounted every two hours, day and night. Rowing galleys were still used between Battersea and Woolwich, while the lower reaches of the river were patrolled by a sailing cutter.

The River Police remained a separate entity until 1839 when they were incorporated into the Metropolitan Police Force and became known as the Thames Division. In 1909, the private police force employed by the various enclosed docks was united with the Port of London Authority in co-operation with the River Police.

Today, a River Policeman must do two years on the beat before s/he can transfer to Thames Division, after which a one-year intensive course is required before taking up service on the river. The fleet of fast cruisers used today is based mainly at Wapping.

DOCKLANDS
Top: *The Port of London in 1842, when steamships began to establish their presence on the Thames.*
Bottom: *The Limehouse Basin, in Docklands.*

A CLOSER LOOK

LONDON BRIDGE

London Bridge has had many incarnations and has suffered many disasters. The current London Bridge was built between 1967 and 1972. Its predecessor, built in 1823-31 by John Rennie, was sold and re-erected at Lake Havasu City, Arizona. Its new owners were disappointed when they saw it; they thought they had bought Tower Bridge.

The first London Bridge, probably wooden, was built between 100 and 400 A.D., during the Roman occupation. By creating the first north-south route to the centre of England from the Continent, the bridge directly influenced the growth of London.

A subsequent bridge was spectacularly destroyed by the Norse King Olaf who had come to help the English King Aethelred against the Danish Vikings. When Olaf tried to take the bridge, stones were dropped onto his ships. He tore down the riverside houses and used the timbers to make protective covers for his oarsmen, then tied ropes to the piles of the bridge and ordered his men to row as hard as they could. The bridge collapsed under its defenders; hence the origin of the nursery rhyme 'London Bridge is Falling Down'.

The first known stone bridge was built in 1176. This medieval bridge was a 'living bridge', with buildings along its length and fortified gates at each end. The heads of traitors (sometimes 30 at a time) were displayed on spikes at the gates as a deterrent. Markets were held on the bridge and at times the congestion was so bad that it could take an hour to cross. To help alleviate the problem, a rule of the road was introduced, making it compulsory for carts and coaches to pass each other to the driver's right.

This bridge had 19 arches and acted like a weir. It was almost impossible to shoot the bridge as the current, whatever the tide, was so strong. In very hard winters the narrow arches caused the river to freeze over and the watermen would organise 'frost fairs' to compensate for their loss of earnings. At one such fair, in 1683-4 and several bridges later, a whole ox was roasted and stalls stretched continuously from the Temple to Southwark.

Frost fairs were impromptu events; official fairs needed a royal charter. Nevertheless, Charles II and his family visited the 1683-4 fair. Hand printing presses had been set up on the ice, and the royal family had their names printed as a memento on a quarto sheet of Dutch paper which is now in the Museum of London.

LONDON BRIDGE AND NONSUCH HOUSE

This first stone bridge was constructed in 1176, with the first mention of houses on the bridge being in 1201.
Nonsuch House was close to the Southwark end and was built entirely of wood, even to the extent
that pegs were used instead of nails.

THE ROYAL WATERMEN

For centuries, watermen have ferried people up, down and across the river in response to the cry of 'Oars!' Since kings first started building palaces on the banks of the Thames they, too, have used the services of watermen, their gilded barges providing an agreeable and rapid means of transport. There is evidence that watermen transported King John by barge to Runnymede, to sign the Magna Carta.

The river was a relatively safe means of travel and there is only one recorded loss of life on a royal barge. In 1264, Eleanor of Provence, wife of Henry III, was being rowed along the Thames when she was stoned by a crowd on London Bridge. The barge sank and one of her ladies of the bedchamber was drowned.

Early in the 14th century, Edward II was protected by his watermen when he was attacked by pirates on the River Fleet. Legend has it that this was when the watermen were given their royal charter and became Royal Watermen.

As the river became busier, it also became more dangerous for passengers. The waterways were congested and, although watermen and lightermen were experienced, the crews of ships awaiting a berth would often act as amateur watermen, despite their lack of knowledge of the local tides or of how to handle small boats. Londoners would also bet on races between watermen, who consequently built narrower and lighter boats which were less safe for their passengers. Watermen were a notoriously rough and bellicose lot, and there was a pressing need for regulation. In 1514, Henry VIII established the Watermen's Company which inspected and licensed boats, regulated apprenticeships, fixed fares and had the power to imprison malefactors or ban them from the river.

The Act passed by Henry also granted a charter to Trinity House to appoint and train pilots throughout England, and to place buoys and lights in estuaries and along the coast.

The Watermen's Hall, originally in Upper Thames Street but now at St Mary-at-Hill near Billingsgate, became the headquarters of the Watermen's Company, where the trade was regulated and rigorous apprenticeships overseen. After apprenticeship, watermen were given arm badges to signify that they had been trained.

Today, the Lord Chamberlain's office appoints Royal Watermen to the Queen for traditional functions such as state processions and escorting the Crown Jewels to the State Opening of Parliament. Although the jewels, like the processions themselves, now travel by road instead of by royal barge, the escort of Royal Watermen is a reminder of the hundreds of years during which the river provided the transport, and of the unique relationship between the Crown, the capital and the Thames.

FACT, FICTION AND FABLE

Winners of Doggett's Coat & Badge Race display their tunics and badges.

Doggett's Coat & Badge Race

Doggett's Coat & Badge Race is the oldest annual sporting event in the country. Intended for six newly apprenticed watermen, it first took place in 1716 and is still contested annually each July, though light sculls have replaced the original heavy skiffs. Competitors row 4½ miles with the flood tide from London Bridge to Cadogan Pier in Chelsea, which takes between forty-five minutes and an hour.

Thomas Doggett, caricatured right performing the 'Cheshire Rounds', was an actor-manager at the Drury Lane Theatre, and his will states that the prize should be 'continued for ever yearly in commemoration of His Majesty King George's happy accession to the British throne'. Another, popular story is that in terrible weather, and rather drunk, Doggett was failing to find a waterman who would row him the 4½ miles against wind and tide to his home in Chelsea. Eventually, a young waterman agreed to take him, and in gratitude Doggett set up the race. He also left money for a prize for the winner: cloth for the livery of a red tunic, and a silver badge.

There is a painting of the first, unnamed, winner in the Watermen's Hall. One of the most famous winners was Jack Broughton (1730). He used boxing to train for rowing, went on to become a champion prize fighter, and was the first to introduce gloves and science into boxing. Broughton Rules were only later superseded by the Queensbury Rules which are used today.

ROYAL WATERMEN

Left: *In an echo of former times, Royal Watermen row Edward Wessex along the Thames in a shallop.*

VAUXHALL

Vauxhall derives its name from Falkes de Breauté who built a house on the south bank of the Thames during the reign of King John. The name has been corrupted through Fulke's Hall, Faukeshall and Foxhall. Vauxhall remained a village throughout the 18th century, but by the 1860s, the village had been engulfed by the houses of Lambeth. Vauxhall Bridge was built in 1816 and replaced in 1895–1906.

VAUXHALL GARDENS
*An exterior view of the gardens
as they looked in 1750,
at which time they were known as
New Spring Gardens.*

A Brief History

c. 1660
The pleasure gardens at Vauxhall, known as the New Spring Gardens until 1785, were opened at about the time of the Restoration in 1660, and became well known as a place of recreation.

1728–67
Jonathan Tyers managed the gardens from 1728 to 1767, and introduced supper boxes, arches, statues, a cascade, a music room, a Chinese pavilion and even an underground orchestra pit. After Frederick, Prince of Wales, attended a masked ball there in 1732, the gardens became a highly fashionable place of entertainment and refreshment. The Prince had his own pavilion in the gardens, where he could be seen entertaining people every night. On some evenings 2,000 people would visit the gardens, causing traffic jams from Lambeth Palace to the entrance.

1749–1827
A number of royal events were held in the gardens. On 21 April 1749 a rehearsal of Handel's Music for the Royal Fireworks attracted an audience of over 12,000; London Bridge was impassable for three hours. 61,000 were attracted to a fancy dress event attended by the Prince of Wales in 1786; in 1813 a grand fête was held to celebrate Wellington's victory at Vittoria, and in 1827 a re-enactment of the Battle of Waterloo took place, involving 1,000 soldiers.

1816
Vauxhall Bridge was opened in 1816, the first iron bridge over the Thames. It was known as 'Regent's Bridge' because its construction was encouraged by the Prince Regent to provide access to Vauxhall Gardens, his favourite haunt.

1859
The gardens closed in 1859 after several 'farewells', the last of which took place on 25 July and included a concert, equestrian performance, dancing and fireworks.

1895–1906
Regent's Bridge was replaced by the present Vauxhall Bridge, designed by Sir Alexander Binnie. The bridge has five steel arches on granite piers with bronze figures representing Pottery, Engineering, Architecture, Agriculture, Science, Fine Arts, Local Government and Education.

A CLOSER LOOK

CLEOPATRA'S NEEDLE

Cleopatra's Needle, on the Victoria Embankment, is the oldest monument in London. It is nearly 60 ft high, weighs 186 tons and was made from granite in Egypt c. 1475 B.C. The obelisk originally stood at Heliopolis, which is now a suburb of Cairo, and was later moved to Alexandria, where it stood for centuries before falling over in the sand.

It was presented to Britain in 1819 by the Turkish Viceroy of Egypt to celebrate Nelson's victory over Napoleon on the Nile. It cost £15,000 to transport and was nearly lost at sea in the Bay of Biscay while being towed in an enormous cylindrical pontoon. Six seamen lost their lives in the gale.

It was eventually erected in 1878 and has a Victorian time capsule buried underneath it containing an odd assortment of objects. These include the day's paper, a set of coins, iron ropes and submarine cable (recently invented), a razor and a box of pins, four bibles in different languages, *Bradshaw's Railway Guide* and photographs of twelve of the best-looking women of the day.

STATUE OF QUEEN BOUDICCA

The statue, commissioned by Queen Victoria, celebrates a legendary rebel leader and national heroine. It was made by Thomas Thornycroft in the 1850s but was not unveiled until 1902.

In 61 A.D. Queen Boudicca led the Iceni tribe against the occupying Romans, attacking London and burning it to the ground. When Emperor Nero's soldiers overwhelmed her forces in 62 A.D., Boudicca took poison rather than fall into her enemy's hands. The legend had a particular resonance in Edwardian Britain, which was experiencing the rise of the suffragette movement.

THE ROYAL HOSPITAL, CHELSEA

A Brief History

1682–92
The Royal Hospital, Chelsea, better known as the Chelsea Hospital, was begun in 1682 as a retirement home for veteran soldiers. It was inspired by the Hôtel des Invalides in Paris, which had been established by Louis XIV earlier in the century. The Chelsea Hospital later inspired Queen Mary's Royal Naval Hospital at Greenwich.

Designed with simplicity and restraint by Christopher Wren, and constructed round three courtyards, the Chelsea Hospital has an air of regal dignity. It is the only one of Wren's buildings for which no plans survive, and it took ten years to build. It was not completed until the reign of William and Mary, so its founder, Charles II, never saw the finished building.

The delay is thought to be due to the fraudulent activities of the Earl of Ranelagh, who had been appointed the army's Paymaster General in 1685. While the hospital was being built, he commissioned Wren to build him a house within

the grounds. He delayed the opening of the Hospital and the admission of the first pensioners until his house was completed, apparently because he was using subscription money for his own house. Ranelagh's misconduct came to light 21 years later and he resigned, after which an independent Board of Commissioners was set up to run the Hospital.

1689
The first 476 pensioners took up residence in 1689, although the building was not completed until 1692. There have also been three women pensioners at Chelsea, the most famous of whom was Hannah Snell.

1852
From 10-17 November 1852 the Duke of Wellington was laid in state at the army's Royal Hospital in Chelsea, just as Nelson had been laid in state at the navy's Royal Hospital in Greenwich. So many people came to pay their last respects to the victor of Waterloo that people were killed in the crush.

The Royal Hospital, Chelsea is the legacy of Charles II. Popular legend has it that Nell Gwynn was responsible for the building, which is romantic but untrue, although she was one of the original patrons and donated £200 to the cause. Funds for the building, which was designed by Christopher Wren, probably came from the King's own pocket and that of his Paymaster General, Sir Stephen Fox.

THE CHELSEA PENSIONERS

The inhabitants of the Royal Hospital are known as Chelsea Pensioners. There are about 420 in-pensioners, who are divided into six companies. Men over 65 (or 55 if they are unable to earn a living) who have been injured in active service are given board, lodging, clothing, a small weekly allowance and nursing care if they are ill.

Pensioners must wear their blue uniforms at all times within a one-mile radius of the Hospital. This uniform includes a peaked cap with the initials RH in red. Further afield, and on special occasions, they wear Ceremonial dress – the familiar scarlet uniform, dating from the 18th century. On special occasions, such as Founder's Day at the end of May, a three-cornered hat is worn.

Founder's Day is celebrated annually on the Saturday nearest the anniversary of Charles II's birth. It is known as Oak Apple Day in deference to the founder, who is reputed to have hidden in an oak tree after the

Battle of Worcester in 1651. The statue of Charles II in the central courtyard is decorated with oak foliage and every pensioner wears an oak sprig. It is the only event at which all pensioners must be present; each must sign a contract stating that they will attend. A member of the current Royal Family is always present on Founder's Day to take the salute and maintain the 300-year tradition. Queen Victoria insisted that half the men facing into the square saluted with their left hand so that she could see the whites of their eyes.

CHELSEA PENSIONERS

Two Chelsea Pensioners stand with Edward Wessex in the Chapel, one of the two main public rooms which Wren designed for the Royal Hospital.

FACT, FICTION AND FABLE

Hannah Snell

Hannah Snell was one of only three women to become a Chelsea Pensioner. She was admitted to the Hospital in 1750, long before the army recruited women, but she had been wounded three times in battle and therefore qualified as an army pensioner.

Hannah, calling herself James Gray and in uniform borrowed from her brother, joined the army in order to search for her husband, a Dutch seaman, who had fathered her child and then disappeared. She had no difficulty getting into the army, for enrolment consisted of kissing the flag, taking the King's shilling and drinking a pint of beer; there was no medical.

Not long after joining her regiment, Hannah was given 500 lashes for allegedly insulting her sergeant. She was not discovered, but deserted, joined the Royal Marines, where she was known as 'Hearty Jemmy', and set sail for the East. It was there that she was wounded, but rather than go to the army surgeon she had a low caste Indian woman dress the wounds.

On her way back to England, Hannah's ship put in at Lisbon, where she learned that her husband had been executed in Genoa. The motive for her martial pursuits was gone, so she discharged herself from the army and set about getting her services and her wounds properly recorded. The Duke of Cumberland secured her an annuity of £30, and she was awarded out-pensioner status at the Chelsea Hospital and given a blue uniform. She never lived at the Hospital but was allowed to wear the uniform, which presumably she did while running her pub in Wapping called 'The Female Warrior'.

Hannah Snell died in London in 1792 and at her own request was laid to rest, in an unmarked grave, among her comrades at the Royal Hospital.

GREENWICH

At one time there were nine royal palaces and residences along the Thames, from Windsor in the west to Greenwich

in the east. Most have sadly disappeared and of the few remaining, only one has retained a clear

association with the river and our country's maritime heritage – Greenwich. Apart from its magnificent setting,

this former palace is blessed with a wonderful history and a number of hidden treasures which make it

a crucial element in the story of Crown and Country.

Furthermore, Greenwich is surrounded by many other examples of the Crown's relationship with the country.

From the royal dockyards at Deptford, to the royal park and royal observatory, and the much older

royal palace at Eltham, there are a wealth of stories and connections. Even across the river we find royal

folklore attached to the mysteriously named Isle of Dogs.

THE ROYAL NAVAL COLLEGE, GREENWICH
This was originally the Royal Naval Hospital, designed by Christopher Wren who gave his services free.
Queen's House can be seen between the two buildings, which at Queen Mary's insistence were built separately
in order that the house would remain visible from the waterfront.

GREENWICH PALACE

A Brief History

1426–1433
The first palace at Greenwich was built in 1426 by Humphrey, Duke of Gloucester, brother of Henry V, and was known as 'Bella Court'. In 1433 the Duke gained permission to enclose 200 acres of land, which now form Greenwich Park.

1445
When Henry VI married Margaret of Anjou, the Duke lent his nephew the palace for their honeymoon. Margaret wanted the house for herself and, soon afterwards, the Duke's wife was accused of witchcraft and the Duke arrested. He died in custody. Margaret took possession of the palace and renamed it 'Placentia'. She introduced many improvements, including glazing the windows, building a treasure house for the royal treasure and the crown jewels, and a pier to allow boats to come and go regardless of the tide.

1491
Henry VIII was born at Greenwich Palace. When he became King, the palace and park became a favourite residence.

1516
Mary I was born at Greenwich Palace.

1533
Elizabeth I was born at Greenwich Palace. As Queen, she used it as her main summer residence.

1553
The young King Edward VI died at the palace.

1613–37
James I gave Greenwich Palace to his queen, Anne of Denmark in 1613. Queen's House was built for her by Inigo Jones from 1616 to 1640.

1642–
The palace fell to ruin under Cromwell. After the Restoration in 1660, Charles II began to rebuild it but it was unfinished at his death; the remains of the Tudor buildings were later demolished to make way for the Royal Naval Hospital.

1696
The present buildings were conceived by Queen Anne as a hospital for retired seamen. They were eventually designed by Christopher Wren for William and Mary, and carried out by Hawksmoor, Vanbrugh and others. The foundation stone was laid at 5 pm on 30 June 1696, the time precisely recorded by the Astronomer Royal, John Flamsteed. Queen Anne contributed the treasure of the notorious pirate Captain Kidd to the foundation; it had been given to the Crown on his arrest.

1869
In 1869, the Hospital ceased to exist, after providing a home for retired seamen for 150 years. It had housed 2,710 'in-pensioners' who lived in wards with everything provided and a shilling a week in their pockets. 'Out-pensions' were also awarded. Discipline was strict but the pensioners were notoriously rowdy and badly behaved; offenders were put into red-sleeved yellow jackets until they were pardoned.

1873–present day
From 1873 until 1997 the buildings were the home of the Royal Naval College, which moved here from Portsmouth. Today, they form part of Greenwich University.

What was until recently the Royal Naval College at Greenwich stands on the site of several earlier palaces. Greenwich Palace was a favourite residence of the Tudor monarchs. It was built by Humphrey, Duke of Gloucester, brother of Henry V, and remained an important royal residence until the Civil War, after which it was demolished to make way for the Royal Naval Hospital.

HUMPHREY, DUKE OF GLOUCESTER

The first palace at Greenwich was built by Humphrey, Duke of Gloucester, brother of Henry V. A soldier prince, like many of the humanists of the Italian Renaissance, he was the first patron of Renaissance learning in England, and named his palace 'Bella Court'. He surrounded himself with scholars and literary men, and built up a private library which later became the nucleus of the Bodleian Library in Oxford.

Humphrey was born on 3 October 1390, the fifth and youngest son of the Earl of Derby (later Henry IV) and his first wife, Mary de Bohun. He was knighted by his father at the age of nine, was nominated a Knight of the Garter the following year, and at the age of twelve he fought at the Battle of Shrewsbury. He is said to have been educated at Balliol College, Oxford, which is thought to be where he developed his love of books and learning.

He was appointed Lord Great Chamberlain in 1413 by his brother, Henry V, and created Earl of Pembroke and Duke of Gloucester in 1414. In 1415 he accompanied Henry to Agincourt, where he was wounded and rescued by Henry after his men had fled, leaving him surrounded by the enemy. Humphrey received many appointments, grants and honours, including Regent of England, and 'Protector and Defender of the Realm and Church of England' after Henry V's death. He continued to play an important part in public affairs for the rest of his life and was a popular figure, earning himself the nickname 'Good Duke Humphrey'.

When his nephew, Henry VI, married Margaret of Anjou (below) in 1445, the Duke lent them Bella Court for their honeymoon. Margaret fell in love with the palace and wanted it for herself. On 18 February 1447 the Duke

was arrested for treason, and died suddenly five days later. He is thought to have been poisoned as great pains were taken to show the public that his body was unmarked. Three men suspected of poisoning him all met violent deaths at the hands of others. The Duke was buried in a tomb which he had prepared for himself in St Albans Abbey, of which he was a benefactor.

A CLOSER LOOK

THE PAINTED HALL

The celebrated ceiling of the Painted Hall in the King William block of the Royal Naval College is the work of James Thornhill. He began work in 1708 and took 19 years to complete the paintings, which include four monarchs, several gods, a tribute to Christopher Wren and a depiction of Time bringing Truth to Light. Four continents are shown; Australia had not yet been discovered. The four seasons are also represented. Thornhill used real models for his paintings, and the model for Winter was the oldest resident of the hospital, Jonathan Varley, who had spent 60 years at sea. He was 96 at the time of the painting and was under observation due to 'lewd and disgusting behaviour'. Thornhill himself is also portrayed, shown holding out his hand in protest at how little he was paid.

The concept for the central part of the painting was a celebration of the liberation of Europe, which was formalised with the Treaty of Utrecht in 1713. William and Mary are shown with a figure representing Europe kneeling at their feet, to whom William is offering the cap of liberty.

In 1805, the Painted Hall was used for the lying-in-state of one of Britain's greatest heroes, Lord Nelson.

NELSON, CHICHESTER AND DRAKE

In December 1805, Lord Nelson lay in state for three days in the Painted Hall at the Royal Naval College in Greenwich. He had been killed in action at the Battle of Trafalgar on 21 October, and his body preserved in brandy and brought back to London. Each night of the lying in state Nelson's body was put in ice in the next room. Finally, he was rowed upriver in the royal barge to be buried in St Paul's Cathedral.

Lord Nelson is not the only British seafaring hero to be associated with Greenwich. On 7 July 1967, Queen Elizabeth II knighted Francis Chichester in front of the Naval College in recognition of his achievement in being the first Englishman to sail single-handed round the world. The ceremony was designed to echo an event which had occurred close to the same spot 386 years earlier, when Queen Elizabeth I knighted Francis Drake after the first ever circumnavigation of the world by an Englishman.

The two Elizabeths knighted the two Francises using the same sword, and both monarchs requested that the vessels these men had sailed in be preserved. Sir Francis Chichester's *Gypsy Moth IV* still survives, after a voyage of 13,750 miles, taking almost exactly nine months, during which time Chichester celebrated his 65th birthday.

Sir Francis Drake's ship, the *Golden Hind*, has long since rotted away: all that remains is wood from the ship that was made into a chair and is now at Buckland Abbey in Devon. But Drake's achievement remains. He set sail from Plymouth in 1577, on board the *Pelican*, with five other ships. After nearly three years, only Drake's ship returned. He renamed her the *Golden Hind* in honour of his patron, Sir Christopher Hatton, whose crest was a golden deer. Drake's feat is all the more remarkable in the light of the fact that he did it without that essential tool of navigation, the ability to calculate longitude.

QUEEN ELIZABETH KNIGHTING SIR FRANCIS
Top: *Elizabeth I knights Francis Drake on the deck of the* Golden Hind *after he became the first Englishman to circumnavigate the globe.*
Bottom: *Elizabeth II knights Francis Chichester in recognition of his achievement in becoming the first Englishman to sail single-handed round the world.*

GREENWICH ROYAL OBSERVATORY

Charles II's Royal Observatory on Greenwich Hill is the oldest scientific institute in Britain. It was set up with the aim of solving the problem of longitude and making navigation less hazardous.

It is built on the site of a watchtower erected by Humphrey, Duke of Gloucester, in 1428, shortly after he had built his palace in Greenwich, Bella Court. The watchtower was used as a summerhouse by Henry VIII, and it was here, during the May Day tournament of 1536, that Anne Boleyn was supposed to have dropped her handkerchief for her lover. The King, looking for any excuse to be rid of her, had her arrested on a charge of adultery, and taken by boat to the Tower.

Sir Christopher Wren designed the Observatory, and the King's Surveyor-General of Ordnance, Sir John Moore, was given the job of overseeing its construction. It was built with surplus bricks from Tilbury Fort, timber and metal salvaged from a demolished gatehouse at the Tower of London, and money raised from the sale of old royal gunpowder.

The foundation stone was laid by the newly appointed (and first) Astronomer Royal, John Flamsteed. He recorded the precise time, 3.14 pm on 10 August 1675, in order that he could cast the horoscope of the building.

The Octagon Room was designed partly for 'a little pompe' and partly to accommodate the long telescopes of the day, but unfortunately, because it had been built on the foundations of a previous building, it did not lie on a true north-south axis and was therefore useless to Flamsteed, who did most of his work in the nearby Sextant House.

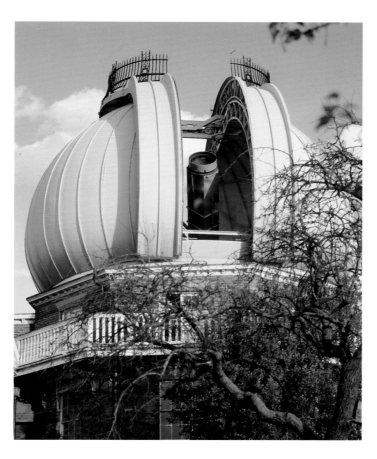

The first accurate measurement of the velocity of light was achieved between the Observatory and a beacon on Shooter's Hill nearby.

On the roof of the Observatory is a pole on which a red ball rises daily at two minutes to 1 pm and drops at exactly 1 pm GMT. This was set up in 1833 as a signal to shipmasters in the Port of London in order that they could set their chronometers accurately.

FACT, FICTION AND FABLE

Longitude

In 1675, Charles II appointed John Flamsteed as the first Astronomer Royal, and set up a Royal Observatory on Greenwich Hill. Flamsteed's brief was to try to solve by astronomy the problem of calculating longitude at sea and so making navigation less hazardous. Forty years later a solution had not been found.

On 22 October 1707, as a result of being unable to establish their position, four royal navy ships were wrecked on Gilstone Ledges off the Scilly Isles, with the loss of over 2,000 lives. This disaster finally brought the longitude problem to public notice.

In 1714, Parliament set up the Board of Longitude, and an enormous prize, of £20,000, was offered to anyone who could solve the problem.

Many weird and wonderful solutions were submitted to the Board. One involved 'Powder of Sympathy', which was purported to be able to heal wounds at long distance by applying the powder to the article which had caused the wound. The cure did, however, cause pain. Every ship was to be equipped with a dog which had been wounded with the same knife; the knife would be kept in London, and at midday, powder of sympathy would be applied to it, causing the dogs to yelp in pain. This would tell the navigator that it was midday in London and, by measuring the position of the sun, he could calculate his longitude.

Crazy though this solution may sound, it shows that being able to determine the time in Greenwich might be one solution to the problem.

John Harrison, a Lincolnshire clockmaker, was convinced of this, and made it his life's work to develop a marine chronometer which would work accurately at sea. It took him 50 years to develop the H4, which lost only five seconds after 62 days at sea, and allowed a navigator to calculate his distance east or west of the meridian by comparing the local time with that at Greenwich.

Harrison had indeed solved the longitude problem but the Government Board, still convinced that the answer must lie in astronomy, refused to award him the prize. Eventually Harrison's son William appealed directly to George III, who intervened. In 1773, Harrison received the money and the recognition which he was owed.

GREENWICH PARK

Greenwich Park is the oldest of the ten royal parks in London. In 1433, Humphrey, Duke of Gloucester, was granted permission to enclose 200 acres of pasture, wood, heath and gorse, and in what is known as the Wilderness there are descendants of the original deer herds which were brought into the park in 1515 for the royal hunt.

However, the origins of the park go back much further than that. The Saxons used to bury their dead in this area, and small mounds still mark the burial site.

Even earlier, there was a Roman temple here, which stood close to what was then Watling Street, the main London to Dover road. Coins have been found here from as early as 425 B.C., and it is thought that travellers may have thrown them down to the temple as an offering. Other theories are that the area was a pay station for soldiers or the home of an officer of the mint.

Remnants of the temple survived until the reign of Elizabeth I, by which time it was little more than a romantic ruin. The area where the temple stood is still known as Queen Elizabeth's Bower.

Henry VIII made the fullest use of the park. On the flat ground he held contests in tilting, shooting at butts, wrestling, fighting with swords and spears, and the curiously sounding 'casting the light and heavy bars'. The athletic young King had special seats set up from which the Queen and young women at court could watch his prowess.

The 'Queen Elizabeth Oak' has been used as a lock-up for those breaking park rules, and tradition has it that Henry VIII danced around the tree with Anne Boleyn.

In 1619, James I enclosed the park with a brick wall, and at the Restoration Charles II had the park redesigned by Le Nôtre who made a focal point of Queen's House. As a result of the arrival of the railway in 1838, the park became a popular place of recreation for Londoners, and Greenwich Fair was held annually in the park during the first part of the 19th century. Up to 250,000 people would come to see attractions which included Mr Richardson's Theatre of clowns, mimes, and snippets of Shakespeare. The fair became so riotous that by 1857 local pressure had it closed down. The existing café and bandstand were built in its place.

A CLOSER LOOK

QUEEN'S HOUSE

Queen's House was commissioned in 1616 by James I for his wife, Anne of Denmark, possibly as a means to ease their troubled relationship. He had already given her Greenwich Palace and the park, in 1613. The house, designed by Inigo Jones, was far from ready when the Queen died in 1619.

Nothing further was done to the building for ten years, until Charles I gave it to his Queen, Henrietta Maria. She asked Inigo Jones to complete the house, which was finished in 1640. With Queen's House, Inigo Jones introduced the Palladian style of architecture to England, though he altered the proportions to make the building longer and lower than its Italian cousins. James I had wanted access from the house to both the river and Greenwich Park, and the house was built straddling the main Deptford to Woolwich road, which passed under a bridge linking the north and south wings.

The house became known as the 'White House' for obvious reasons, and 'The House of Delights' because Henrietta preferred it to any of the other royal residences.

Inside, the Great Hall is a perfect cube and a precursor of Jones's cube rooms at the Banqueting House at Whitehall Palace and Wilton House near Salisbury. The famous iron open-well 'Tulip' staircase, the first of its kind in Britain, rises to the skylight with no central support. Outside, a loggia looks out over the park.

Henrietta Maria was forced to leave the house in 1642 with the outbreak of the Civil War, and the house was taken over by the Parliamentarians. The Queen returned to the house after the Restoration, and in 1662 John Webb, a pupil of Inigo Jones, added two first-floor rooms for her.

From 1690 Queen's House was used by successive Rangers of Greenwich Park until 1710 when it was used by the governors of the Naval Hospital. Between 1730 and 1737 Caroline of Ansbach, queen of George II, took over the house, after which time the house was once again used by the Ranger of the Park, Lady Catherine Pelham.

In 1795 Caroline of Brunswick was received at Queen's House on her arrival in England to marry the Prince of Wales, later George IV. In 1805 Caroline was appointed Ranger and was granted the house. It was sold in 1806 to the Royal Naval Asylum as a school for sailor's orphans. In 1809 colonnades were added to commemorate the Battle of Trafalgar.

The school moved to Suffolk in 1933 and Queen's House was left in a bad condition. It was restored in 1933-35 by the Office of Works, and opened in 1937 as part of the National Maritime Museum. Further restoration took place between 1984-90.

ST ALFEGE'S CHURCH

The original church in Greenwich High Road was built by the Saxons and dedicated to Alfege, Archbishop of Canterbury, who was martyred on the site of the church on 19 April 1012. Alfege had been taken prisoner by Danes when they invaded in 1011, and was brought in chains from Canterbury to the fortified village of Greenwich, where the main Danish force was camped on Blackheath.

He tried to escape but was recaptured in the boggy marshland. As a punishment, his ransom was raised to £51,000 but Alfege told the English not to pay it: the diocese was poor and the Danes were known not to keep their word. A week later, drunken Danes celebrating Easter began to pelt Alfege with ox bones left over from their feast. A man called Thrum, whom Alfege had converted, took pity on him and, to save him from further suffering, administered the final blow with an axe.

The Saxon church was rebuilt in the 13th century, and Henry VIII was baptised at St Alfege's in 1491.

Today's church was designed by Nicholas Hawksmoor and was also the first to be built under the 50 New Churches Act of 1711, which was instigated by Queen Anne to accommodate a growing London population. The present church was consecrated in 1718, and restored, after bombing, in 1952.

The composer Thomas Tallis was buried at St Alfege's in 1585, and his music is played at Evensong every 23 November, the anniversary of his death.

THE ROYAL NAVAL DOCKYARD AT DEPTFORD

Deptford (or Depeford), Rotherhithe and Erith, on the south bank of the Thames, all boasted substantial shipyards from Tudor times onwards.

Henry VIII's Royal Naval Dockyard at Deptford, in what was then a fishing village, became known as 'The Cradle of the Navy'. The King's giant flagship, the *Great Harry*, was built in Woolwich, fitted out in Erith, and launched at Greenwich in 1514.

According to legend, it was close to the master shipwright's building in Deptford that Sir Walter Raleigh famously laid down his cloak for Elizabeth I, to prevent her from getting her feet wet.

Captain Cook's ships, the *Resolution*, *Adventure* and *Discovery*, were all equipped here for his voyages to the Pacific.

Perhaps the most unusual visitor to Deptford was Peter the Great, Czar of Russia, who was invited to England by William III in 1698 to learn about naval shipbuilding. The Czar stayed at Sayes Court, the grace and favour home of the diarist John Evelyn. Evelyn had spent 45 years laying out his 100-acre estate, and his pride and joy was a 400 ft holly hedge, 9 ft high and 5 ft wide. The Czar and his friends (one of whom was Edmond Halley, the second Astronomer Royal) managed to wreck much of the house and the beautiful gardens: one of their favourite pranks was to push each other at full speed through the holly hedge in a wheelbarrow!

The Czar was, however, a good student. He learned enough English to preach at the Quaker church near the dock gates, and on his return to Russia put his new shipbuilding skills into practice by establishing a naval fleet. Deptford's coat-of-arms shows the Czar sitting on a stool, using an adze to shape a piece of wood.

In 1832, after the conclusion of the wars with France, the Royal Dockyard was closed. Five years later it reopened, and its last ship, the *Druid*, was launched in 1869, after which the work of the Deptford yard was transferred to Chatham and Sheerness.

The dockyard and the Royal Victoria Victualling Yard on its west side were subsequently used as a cattle market; they are now in use as docks again, handling huge container ships carrying paper from Scandinavia.

DEPTFORD
Left: *Sir Walter Raleigh laying down his cloak for Elizabeth I.*
Below: *Peter the Great, Czar of Russia, studying shipbuilding at Deptford Dockyard.*

A CLOSER LOOK

THE ISLE OF DOGS

The marshland of the low-lying peninsula on the great bend of the Thames opposite Greenwich has been drained on several occasions since medieval times. In the 17th century, windmills were erected to help reclaim land, and in 1805 a canal was cut across the neck of the peninsula as part of the newly built West India Docks. The 'Isle' finally became an island.

There are three theories about the derivation of the name, the Isle of Dogs. One is that it is a pun on the name of a 16th-century landowner called Brache, which was a kind of hunting dog. A more elaborate theory is based on the tragic story of a young nobleman and his bride who celebrated their wedding by going hunting. The bride and her horse became separated from the rest, and strayed into the marshy swamp where they became trapped and drowned. Her husband, searching in vain, ventured too far into the bog where he also died. Their dogs, left on the shoreline, became increasingly uneasy and began howling for their master. The Isle of Dogs is even today supposed to be haunted by ghostly huntsmen and a pack of phantom hounds.

However, the most likely explanation of the name is that the island was used to kennel the royal hunting pack when the King resided at Greenwich.

It is said that pirates used to be hanged on the foreshore of the island opposite Greenwich Hospital, and that the pensioners would hire out spyglasses to interested visitors.

THE *MAYFLOWER*

The 'Mayflower' pub in Rotherhithe is named after the ship which took the Pilgrim Fathers to America, where they established a colony in 1620.

Captain Christopher Jones moored the *Mayflower* nearby, and the crew, most of whom were local, met at the pub (then known as 'The Shippe') before setting sail to join the *Speedwell* at Southampton, with its complement of Puritans from East Anglia.

The two ships set sail in convoy, but 200 miles out, the *Speedwell* sprang a leak and they headed back to land. The *Speedwell* was abandoned in Plymouth and the *Mayflower* set sail again, with the passengers of both ships, returning to London in 1621. Christopher Jones died in Rotherhithe and is buried in the graveyard of St Mary's Church opposite the pub.

'The Shippe' was rebuilt in the 18th century and renamed the 'Spread Eagle and Crown'. In the second half of the 20th century it was again renamed, to commemorate the *Mayflower*.

The pub is one of a very few inns licensed to sell English postage stamps; in honour of its connection with America, it is also licensed to sell American stamps. A model of the *Mayflower* hangs outside the entrance.

ELTHAM PALACE

Several Tudor monarchs, including Henry VIII, were born at Greenwich Palace and spent much of their childhood a few miles further south at Eltham Palace. More recently, the Palace was leased by English Heritage and is now open to the public.

HENRY VIII

Henry was born at Greenwich Palace on 28 June 1491, the second son of Henry VII and Elizabeth of York. He spent much of his childhood at Eltham Palace, which remained a favourite residence during the early part of his reign. But his relationship with Eltham, as with his wives and the country as a whole, did not remain constant.

Few kings have set out so consciously to glorify the style and splendour of the monarchy: Henry was the first to be addressed as 'Majesty'. Holbein's portrait of the King catches the majesty of his bearing. He is the best known of the English monarchs, largely because of his six wives: 'divorced, beheaded, died; divorced, beheaded, survived'.

Yet the young Henry was handsome, intelligent and athletic, and added to his popularity by executing his father's hated tax collectors, Empson and Dudley. He left Cardinal Wolsey in charge of mundane administration, allowing him such power that many people thought Wolsey was actually running the country. Meanwhile, Henry wasted resources on flamboyant but unsuccessful campaigns against France, Scotland and Spain. He recouped vast amounts of money by dissolving the monasteries and confiscating their property, which was seen by many as the act of a megalomaniac royal vandal but by others as freeing ordinary people from the feudalism of the church. Ironically, Henry had already earned the title *Fidei Defensor*, Defender of the Faith, from the Pope; it appears as FD on British coins to this day.

The tragedy of Henry VIII lies in the fact that his intelligence, drive and ability – qualities which could have made him a truly great king – were his undoing. Encouraged by the adulation and flattery of his courtiers and companions, the very characteristics which made him the 'Bluff King Hal' of his youth, turned into an overwhelming sense of superiority over his fellow men. The country could only watch as Henry metamorphosed from 'the perfect Renaissance prince' into the ogre of his later years – egotistical, bloated and despotic.

Henry was a prolific appropriator of castles and builder of palaces. By the time of his death he had accumulated over 60 residences; more than any other monarch has ever owned.

ELTHAM PALACE

Above: *The curved colonnade and staircase pavilions of the Courtauld house which was designed by Seeley and Paget in the 1930s.*
Below: *A detail of the exterior wall of the Great Hall.*
When the hall was built in the 1470s it was second in size only to Westminster Hall.

FACT, FICTION AND FABLE

The Order of the Garter

In 1348, Edward III returned triumphantly to England from fighting in France. It is thought that it was while he was at Eltham Palace that he founded the Order of the Garter, the oldest and highest order of chivalry in Europe. The Order was originally limited to the Sovereign, Prince of Wales and 24 knights. The fact that George III had seven sons, however, presented a problem, and in 1786 a statute allowed them supernumerary status. The only Ladies of the Garter are the Sovereign's queen and their eldest daughter when she is heir apparent.

The insignia are a mantle, surcoat, hood, star, collar, George (a jewelled figure of St George and the dragon), a diagonal blue ribbon and the garter, to be worn below the left knee. Knights are entitled to put the letters KG after their name.

The popular legend is that Edward stooped to pick up the garter of Joan, Countess of Salisbury, who dropped it at a court ball. He rebuked his laughing courtiers by saying, *Honi soit qui mal y pense*: evil (or shame) be to him who thinks evil of it, which remains the motto of the Order.

Until 1862, Knights of the Garter were selected by a form of election. Each existing member of the Order would vote for nine candidates, from whom the sovereign would choose as many as were needed to fill any vacancies. Shortly after the death of Prince Albert, Queen Victoria announced that she no longer felt able to attend elections. Since then appointments have been made by Royal Prerogative, the matter being formalised by a Garter Statute in 1953.

The spiritual home of the Order is St George's Chapel Windsor, where each Knight's banner, helm, crest and sword is set above his stall in the quire.

ELTHAM PALACE

Above: *The 1930s Dining Room where the Courtaulds had dinner served at 8 pm from a French menu and accompanied by vintage wine.*

Right: *The Entrance Hall today, where beneath the spectacular glass-domed ceiling exact replicas of furniture from the period have been reproduced from Courtauld family photographs and inventories.*

BLACKHEATH

A Brief History

1381
Wat Tyler, leader of the Peasants' Revolt, mustered his rebels on Blackheath. The fourteen-year-old King, Richard II, was prevented from meeting or negotiating with the rebels, with the result that Tyler's Kentish band ransacked Southwark, Fleet Street, the Temple and the City, while Richard II reached agreement with rebels from Essex, encamped at Mile End.

1415
Henry V was welcomed here on his triumphant return from the Battle of Agincourt.

1431
Henry VI was greeted at Blackheath after his coronation in Paris as King of France, which took place two years after his coronation as King of England at Westminster Abbey.

1450
Jack Cade, the leader of the Kentish Rebellion, a seemingly spontaneous uprising in protest at the oppression of the lower classes and the corrupt and incompetent government of Henry VI, used Blackheath as a sounding-board for his grievances. The rebels entered London on 3 July but then Cade lost control of his followers, who were expelled from the City. The rebels were camped on Blackheath when they were persuaded to accept pardons and disperse.

1497
The Battle of Blackheath in 1497 is the only battle to have taken place here. The Cornish Rebellion against taxes levied by Henry VII took the form of a march on London led by Michael Joseph. At Blackheath, the rebels were met by the King's army and the rebellion was crushed.

1540
A huge pageant was staged at Blackheath when Henry VIII went there to meet his future bride, Anne of Cleves.

1608
A Society of Blackheath Golfers was formed; the game was played close to Greenwich Palace. James I's Scottish courtiers had introduced the game to London.

1660
Charles II was welcomed at Blackheath on his return from France at the Restoration.

18th century
George I and George II both reviewed their troops on Blackheath.

1858
Blackheath FC was founded by former pupils of Blackheath Proprietary School and is the oldest rugby club in London. Blackheath FC was one of the founder members of the Rugby Union in 1871.

Blackheath lies on the route from London to Canterbury and Dover. It takes its name not from victims of the black death, as local legend suggests, but from what lies beneath the surface: black peat. Events that have occurred on the heath are divided between royal pageantry and revolts against the crown.

CAROLINE OF BRUNSWICK

In 1795, Caroline of Brunswick arrived at Greenwich en route to marry her cousin, the Prince of Wales, later George IV. She had an inauspicious welcome, being greeted by Lady Jersey, a known mistress of the Prince.

George had been pressurised into the marriage for political and financial reasons and was already secretly married to Maria Fitzherbert. It is said that he only managed to get through the ceremony by being blind drunk, and within weeks, the Prince and Princess were living apart, although by that time Caroline was already pregnant with Princess Charlotte, who was born in 1796.

Caroline was infuriated by the constant presence of Lady Jersey and rented Montague House in Blackheath, where she became involved in local life and was appointed Ranger of the Park. Caroline was barred from George's coronation but, through all her troubles, the people of Greenwich stood by her, writing letters of support and declaring their love for her.

The Princess was an eccentric, which did not endear her to the Court where she was the subject of vindictive gossip. She became involved with the running of an orphanage where her interest in one boy, William Austin, fuelled rumours that he was her illegitimate son. In 1806 an Inquiry was set up which became known as the Delicate Investigation. No evidence could be found against Caroline but she never regained her reputation.

Caroline's behaviour became increasingly bizarre and amongst other things she was known to bathe outside in a specially constructed bath which stood in the grounds of Montague House.

BLACKHEATH
Far left: *The Peasants' Revolt: Wat Tyler's mob burn St John's monastery near Smithfield after gathering at Blackheath.*
Left: *Henry VIII came to meet Anne of Cleves at Blackheath.*
Below: *A view across the heath towards the neo-gothic Church of All Saints, built in 1858.*

THE CITY

While Westminster has always been the administrative centre of the kingdom, the commercial centre has always

been the City. Situated at the heart of our sprawling capital, the City of London has its distinct culture,

way of life, traditions, customs and even its own police force. Built on trade and tradesmen, money and dealing,

the City has long been the most important financial influence on the development of the country,

a fact which has demanded a special relationship with the Crown.

Time and again we see examples of this relationship through the stories of the Corporation of London, the Livery

Companies, the Lord Mayors, the Bank of England, the Royal Exchange and that great symbol of London, St

Paul's Cathedral. Even the Bishops of London have a unique link with the Crown as Deans of the Chapel Royal.

Of all the major events which underline this relationship, the most tragic must be the Great Fire of London.

ST PAUL'S CATHEDRAL
*The dome of St Paul's, second in size only to St Peter's in Rome,
towers above another London icon, the Routemaster bus.*

ST PAUL'S CATHEDRAL

Britain's only classical cathedral, St Paul's Cathedral is the masterpiece of one of England's finest architects, Sir Christopher Wren. The building is a towering monument to Wren's genius and determination, and became a symbol of hope and defiance for Londoners during the Blitz.

ST PAUL'S CATHEDRAL

Edward Wessex in front of St Paul's. The marble statue of Queen Anne is by Richard Belt (1886)
and is a copy of a statue by Francis Bird which was erected in 1712, to commemorate the completion of the cathedral,
but which deteriorated badly.

A Brief History

1240 B.C.
St Paul's is reputed to stand on the site of a pagan temple built in 1240 B.C. by Brutus, London's mythical Trojan founder. According to the 10th-century cleric Geoffrey of Monmouth, Brutus was the great-grandson of Aeneas and came eventually to Albion, which he renamed Britain after his own name.

881–61 B.C.
Geoffrey of Monmouth states that Bladud, the ancient founder of Bath and ruler of Britain for twenty years, crash-landed a magical flying stone on this site! Bladud's successor was his son Leir who reigned for sixty years, and was the model for Shakespeare's King Lear. He, in turn, was succeeded by his daughter, Cordelia.

Roman Britain
There was a Roman temple to Diana on the site of the cathedral.

c. 604 A.D.
The first cathedral on the site was built c. 604 by King Ethelbert of Kent, the first Christian king in England, for Bishop Mellitus, the first Bishop of London. It was dedicated to St Paul, the patron saint of the City of London.

675–962
The first cathedral burnt down and a new St Paul's was built between 675 and 685 by Bishop Eorconweald, the fourth Bishop of London. This second cathedral was destroyed by the Vikings in 962.

1087
The third Saxon church was destroyed by fire in 1087, and immediately after this the Normans set about building a church which would reflect the importance of their newly conquered kingdom. Built of Caen stone brought by sea from Normandy, it became the largest building in England and the third largest church in Europe, with the tallest spire ever built. Old St Paul's, as it was subsequently known,

was considerably larger and taller than the present cathedral.

1285
The cathedral precincts were enclosed by walls in 1285 to keep out robbers and marauders.

14th century
Old St Paul's became the focal point for processions, ceremonies and services of thanksgiving, as well as being an attraction to pilgrims, with its rich and precious shrines. Street traders, using St Paul's as a cut-through between Carter Lane and Paternoster Row with their animals and wares, were attracted by the crowds, and set up stalls in the precinct.

1385
Activity in the cathedral became so boisterous that in 1385 it became necessary to ban ball games. For several centuries, services were conducted in the quire against a background of tradesmen's noisy activity.

1415
Henry V prayed and made offerings in the cathedral before embarking to fight the French. From the cathedral steps, the Bishop read out news of the victory at Agincourt, and a month later the King gave thanks at the cathedral.

1501
On 14 November, the wedding took place of Arthur, Prince of Wales, and Princess Catherine of Aragon, who was later to marry Arthur's younger brother, Henry VIII.

16th century
The Reformation, precipitated by Henry VIII's divorce of Catherine, meant that the Dean and the Chapter could no longer afford to maintain the fabric of the building. Traders set up their stalls on the tombs and font, horse fairs were held in the nave, lawyers received their clients there, and servants were hired. The nave became known as St Paul's Walk, and was effectively an extension of Cheapside market.

1558–1603
Elizabeth I was a generous benefactor to the cathedral, and regularly attended Protestant services there, interrupting the service if she disagreed with something or had heard enough. In 1588, she arrived in a chariot drawn by white horses for a thanksgiving service to celebrate the defeat of the Spanish Armada; it was said that the Queen's procession was like a second coronation.

1561
On 4 June 1561, fire again played a part in the cathedral's history. The magnificent spire was struck by lightning, caught fire and was totally destroyed, along with the roof. Elizabeth I gave a large donation and allocated timber from the royal forests for rebuilding work, but repairs were makeshift and the spire was never replaced. The slow but steady decline of St Paul's continued.

1569
In 1569, the first public lottery was held at the west door of the cathedral, but the funds raised were used for the repair of the kingdom's harbours rather than the cathedral.

1638–49
Charles I authorised extensive repairs by the King's Surveyor, Inigo Jones. Jones cleared the precincts of the shops and houses that had been built right up to the cathedral walls, and made improvements to the cathedral itself with money from the Privy Purse. But work was halted by the Civil War, and the money in the restoration fund was used by Cromwell to pay his forces. The nave became a cavalry barracks, and by the end of the war, the cathedral and the bishop's palace had been wrecked by the Parliamentarian troops.

September 1666
After the Restoration, Charles II intended to restore St Paul's, and plans were already being considered when the cathedral was destroyed in the

Great Fire of London. All that was left was a heap of stones bound together by the lead which had covered the roof. Christopher Wren was commissioned to build a new St Paul's cathedral but funds only became available for the rebuilding in 1670; these were raised largely by taxing all the coal that came into London.

1675
The foundation stone of the new cathedral was laid on 21 June 1675. Grinling Gibbons was responsible for many of the carvings in the new cathedral. Sir James Thornhill designed the frescoes in the dome.

1711
St Paul's was declared complete in 1711. The building of the new cathedral had spanned the reign of four monarchs but was completed within the episcopy of one Bishop of London, Henry Compton.

1795
Wren had wanted no monuments in his cathedral. However, in 1795, the first one was erected, in memory of the pioneer Quaker prison reformer, John Howard; there are now over 300 tombs in the cathedral.

1939-45
In the Second World War, the cathedral stood as a beacon of hope during the Blitz of London, and miraculously remained unscathed – due in large part to the St Paul's Watch. It became a symbol of hope and resistance to the nation.

1981
The marriage of Charles, Prince of Wales, and Lady Diana Spencer was celebrated at the cathedral on 29 July 1981: the second royal wedding to have taken place in the cathedral.

THE GREAT FIRE OF LONDON

The most destructive fire that England had ever seen started on the night of 1 September 1666 in Thomas Faryner's bakehouse on Pudding Lane, and raged for almost a week. While most of London was sleeping, the fire that was to devastate so much of the city was quietly smouldering.

In 1666, the City of London was cramped and overcrowded, and its citizens weakened by the continuing Great Plague which had killed 70,000 people, reaching its height the previous year. The summer had been long and hot, and the wooden buildings of the city were tinder dry.

When the fire was first spotted, it was thought that it would burn itself out. At 3 am, the Lord Mayor, Sir Thomas Bloodworth, was summoned to the scene but dismissed the fire as insignificant and went back to bed. His lack of interest fatally delayed the organisation of a fire-fighting force; within four hours, the fire was starting to take hold and those living nearby were frantically gathering their possessions and fleeing the city. At 10 am, the Lord Mayor was called out again but was reluctant to pull down houses as a firebreak; he thought the cost of rebuilding them would be too high!

Samuel Pepys was a witness both to the fire and to the Lord Mayor's reluctance to act. As a government official, he took matters into his own hands and went straight to the King, who ordered the Lord Mayor to pull down houses. By this time the blaze was a mile long and a strong south-east wind was fanning the flames. By Tuesday 4 September, it had reached St Paul's and the roof of the great cathedral cascaded down in a torrent of molten lead.

When the fire finally burned itself out on 6 September, the city was a blackened ruin. Not only had St Paul's been razed to the ground but so had the Royal Exchange, Newgate Gaol, Bridewell, the Custom House, 13,200 houses, 87 parish churches, 6 chapels, 52 livery companies, 3 city gates and 4 stone bridges. It was estimated that £10 million worth of damage had been done at a time when the annual income of the city was £12,000.

The 10,000 Londoners who had been made homeless were afraid to return and were camping outside the city walls. Rumours were spreading that the fire had been started deliberately as part of a foreign plot, and Charles II rode among the citizens, trying to allay fears that they were about to be stormed by the Dutch and the French, and encouraging them to return to their homes. In April of that year, Papists had been arrested for plotting to burn down the city on 3 September because the stars had predicted a major disaster for that day. Frenchmen, Dutchmen and Roman Catholics were now locked up for their own safety.

There were surprisingly few casualties of the fire but one indirect victim was a Frenchman called Robert Hubert, who confessed, in a rather confused state, to starting the fire. He was tried and found guilty, even though his story was inconsistent and obviously untrue. Thomas Faryner, the baker, added his signature to the death warrant, presumably to remove the blame from his own shoulders, and the young Frenchman was hanged in October 1666. Three months later, an official parliamentary inquiry decided that the fire had been started accidentally.

The Monument was erected as a lasting memorial to the events of September 1666. A simple Doric column topped with an urn of flames, it was designed by Christopher Wren and his friend Robert Hooke, and constructed of Portland stone, from 1671-7. A balcony beneath the urn can be reached by a spiral staircase of 311 steps. The Monument is the tallest isolated stone column in the world – its height of 202 ft is the same distance as it stands from where the fire started.

FACT, FICTION AND FABLE

Samuel Pepys

Pepys's famous diary covers the years 1660 to 1669. It gives a dramatic description of the Great Fire of London, and of Pepys's own part in it, and records the gossip and scandal of Charles II's court, theatrical life, and public events such as the Plague and the enemy Dutch fleet sailing up the Thames. It also describes Pepys's own domestic life and his problems at work.

Born in 1633, Pepys worked for the Admiralty throughout most of his life, rising to be secretary to the Navy Board, where he worked with industry and efficiency. Responsible for supplies during the Dutch War of 1664-7, he waged a continuous struggle against corrupt officials and dishonest contractors. In 1679 he was briefly imprisoned in the Tower of London, one of many falsely accused in the Popish plot, and only returned to his job in 1684. He was elected president of the Royal Society in the same year. He died in 1703.

THE MONUMENT

Above: *The Monument is the same height as the distance it stands from where the Great Fire of London started in Pudding Lane.*

Right: *The west panel of the pedestal, showing a bas-relief by Caius Gabriel Cibber. This is an allegorical design showing Charles II in Roman costume, accompanied by the Duke of York, commanding his attendants to bring relief to the city.*

FACT, FICTION AND FABLE

Sir Christopher Wren

Christopher Wren is probably the greatest architect England has known, and his career spanned the reigns of seven monarchs from Charles I to George I. He was born in 1632 and although trained in mathematics, physics and astronomy, Wren turned to architecture in the 1660s, and was responsible for, among many other buildings, the Sheldonian Theatre and the Ashmolean Museum in Oxford; the library at Trinity College, Cambridge; the Royal Exchange, the College of Physicians, the Royal Hospital, Chelsea and part of Westminster Abbey in London; and the Royal Observatory and Hospital in Greenwich.

The Great Fire of London provided him with his greatest opportunity, and although his scheme for rebuilding the entire City was thwarted, he nevertheless built 52 City churches, and, of course, St Paul's.

With others, Wren founded the Royal Society in the 1650s, and became president in 1680. He was knighted in 1673; in 1684 he was made Comptroller of Windsor Castle, and in 1698 Surveyor General of Westminster Abbey. He died in 1723.

CHRISTOPHER WREN'S ST PAUL'S

It took several years for Wren's designs for the new St Paul's to be accepted. His first design, in 1669, was rejected, so for his second, in 1673, he produced a beautiful model, costing £600, which is still kept at the Cathedral. Charles II approved it, and Wren was knighted two days later; but it was vetoed by the clergy, who were horrified by the huge dome and classical design, and complained that the nave and the quire were too short.

Wren is said to have burst into tears on its rejection, but he was determined to build the cathedral of his dreams. For his third design, in 1674, he produced a compromise which he knew his critics would approve. It was given the royal warrant but included a clause, of which Wren took full advantage, allowing him to make 'rather ornamental than essential' variations; as the Cathedral rose, it gradually took on the shape of the rejected second model.

WREN'S MODEL OF ST PAUL'S

This is Wren's second design for St Paul's, which was approved by Charles II but vetoed by the clergy. Wren is said to have burst into tears on its rejection, but it is clear that the Cathedral as it was actually built came close to this second design.

In order to demolish the remains of the old cathedral quickly, Wren began by using dynamite, but the residents of Ludgate Hill panicked, thinking there had been an earthquake, and he resorted to battering rams instead. When the site was clear, Wren asked a labourer to bring him a stone to act as a marker for the exact centre of the dome. A flat stone was brought from a nearby heap of rubble, and when Wren turned it over, he found that it was part of a gravestone from the old cathedral, inscribed with the single Latin word, *resurgam* – 'I shall rise again'. On 21 June 1675 this stone was laid as the foundation stone of the new St Paul's.

The incident so impressed Wren that he had the word carved into the fabric of the cathedral, where it can still be seen above the great south door, beneath an image of the phoenix rising from the flames.

For the next 22 years, Wren supervised the work, scrutinised and signed the accounts, engaged the finest craftsmen and visited the site every Saturday by wherry from his lodgings across the river. Between visits, he watched progress through a telescope from his room.

The quire was opened on 2 December 1697 for a service of thanksgiving, and on 5 December the first Sunday service was held in the new cathedral. However, the dome had yet to be built. Nearly ten years later, huge tarred cloths were put up, and for the next two years work continued with an air of secrecy. Wren was hauled up in a basket two or three times a week to see how work was progressing. When the dome was finally revealed, the citizens looked in awe at the magnificence which now crowned the London skyline. By this time Wren was an old man, and not strong enough to lay the last stone, so his son was winched up to the top of the dome to fix it in place on the lantern at the top of the cupola.

In 1697 when the quire was opened, parliament decreed that work was progressing too slowly and reduced Wren's annual salary by half, until the cathedral was completed. The exact date of completion is uncertain; Wren's son records that he laid the last stone in 1710, but it was not until the end of 1711 that parliament declared the cathedral complete, 36 years after the laying of the foundation stone. Wren only received his arrears by making a personal appeal to Queen Anne, by which time he was eighty.

In 1723, twelve years after the completion of the cathedral, Wren was helped up the steps of St Paul's by his coachman. Nobody seemed to notice him as he sat beneath the dome, a frail old man of ninety-one watching the play of sunlight on the stonework of his masterpiece. Later, he slowly hobbled away, and that afternoon he died. He was one of the first people to be buried in the crypt and has a simple black stone with the inscription *Lector, si monumentum requiris circumspice* – 'Reader, if you need a monument, look around you.'

FACT, FICTION AND FABLE

Henry Compton

Henry Compton was born in 1632. He was Bishop of London throughout the rebuilding of St Paul's. An ex-royalist cavalry commander, he is thought to be the last bishop to have donned armour. Compton left several legacies for posterity, including the St Paul's Cathedral library: in his will on his death in 1713, he bequeathed 2,000 rare books and manuscripts to the library, which has remained virtually unchanged since it was completed in 1709. The oldest book is the service book which was used in Old St Paul's and which was written over 800 years ago. The rarest is the first edition of Tyndale's New Testament of 1525, which is one of only two in the world.

From the 11th century until 1973, Fulham Palace was the out-of-city residence of the Bishops of London. The gardens of the palace became famous for their trees when Compton, mentor to the churches being set up in the colonies of America, became bored with letters about church life and asked for seeds and cuttings to be sent instead. Descendants of some of these trees survive today, though the palace is now in the public domain.

The Bishop of London is third in the church hierarchy after the Archbishops of Canterbury and York. The first Bishop of London was Bishop Mellitus, for whom the original St Paul's Cathedral was built in 604 by Ethelbert, King of Kent. Ethelbert also bestowed on Mellitus the manor of Tillingham, Kent, which is still in the possession of the Dean and Chapter. The current Bishop of London is the 132nd incumbent.

Grinling Gibbons

Grinling Gibbons, woodcarver and sculptor, was born in 1648 in Holland but worked in Britain, where he attracted the attention of John Evelyn who introduced him to Sir Christopher Wren. Gibbons was appointed to the Board of Works by Charles II, and was 'master carver' under five British sovereigns. He specialised in carving fruit and flower motifs. Much of his work was done for the royal palaces, but his work can also be seen on the quire stalls and organ screen of St Paul's, and in houses such as Chatsworth and Burghley. He died in 1720.

Sir James Thornhill

Thornhill was born in 1675 in Melcombe Regis, Dorset, for which he later became the Member of Parliament. He executed baroque paintings for the dome of St Paul's, the hall at Blenheim Palace, Hampton Court, and the Painted Hall at Greenwich Hospital. It is said that one day, while inspecting his work on St Paul's Cathedral dome, he stepped back to inspect the effect of his work and was so close to the edge that his assistant was afraid to shout out a warning. Instead, he began to smear the painting, making Thornhill spring forward in fury, and thus saving him from probable death. Thornhill also painted portraits and founded a drawing school. Hogarth, one of his pupils, became his son-in-law. Thornhill was knighted in 1720 by George I and appointed Sergeant-Painter; in 1728 he became history painter to the King. He died in 1734.

A CLOSER LOOK

HORATIO·VISC·NELSON

HORATIO, VISCOUNT NELSON

Lord Nelson's tomb (left) is directly beneath the central point of the great dome of the cathedral. His coffin was made from the mainmast of the French flagship, *L'Orient*, and lies inside a black marble casket which was made for Cardinal Wolsey and confiscated by Henry VIII. It lay forgotten at Windsor Castle until Nelson's body was brought back from Trafalgar to lie in state in the Painted Hall at Greenwich Hospital. Although Lord Nelson's funeral at St Paul's in 1806 was a state occasion, there was no royal representative; George III refused to attend because he disapproved so strongly of Nelson's liaison with Lady Hamilton.

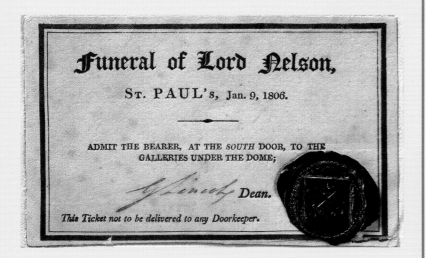

Horatio Nelson was born on 29 September 1758, one of eight children. Nelson's father, Edmund, was rector at Burnham Thorpe in Norfolk, and Edmund's pastoral duties brought the young Horatio into daily contact with the underprivileged, instilling in him a humanity for which he became renowned. He had some formal schooling, and in 1770, at the age of 12, joined HMS *Raisonnable*, commanded by his uncle, Captain Maurice Suckling. Nelson's rise through the ranks was meteoric, leading to his promotion to Rear Admiral in 1797 for his part in the Battle of Cape St Vincent; his courage and skill during this battle brought him a knighthood and made him a national hero, but it was also where he lost his right arm. In 1789, he destroyed the French fleet almost entirely in the Battle of the Nile; in 1801 he was promoted to Vice Admiral and sent to the Baltic, where he won a decisive victory over the Danes at the Battle of Copenhagen and was created a viscount on his return; in 1803 he was given command of the British fleet in the Mediterranean, which culminated in his famous defeat of the combined French and Spanish fleets on 21 October 1805 off Cape Trafalgar, where he was mortally wounded.

ST PAUL'S IN THE BLITZ

The night of 8 September 1940 was to mark the start of events which had a more devastating effect on London than the Great Fire of 1666. For 76 consecutive nights, apart from 2 November when bad weather grounded the Luftwaffe, London was bombarded from the air in the Blitz.

The devastation was immense but the spirit of Londoners would not be broken. Many of the capital's buildings were destroyed or badly damaged: London was an easy target, with the bombers guided in by even the smallest glimmer of moonlight reflecting from the Thames. St Paul's was particularly vulnerable because of its proximity to the Thames, but was miraculously unharmed, in spite of an unexploded bomb burying itself under the south-west tower. Among the fire and rubble all around, St Paul's stood out as a beacon of hope and survival 'like a great ship lifting above the smoke and flame'.

Churchill sent a message to the Lord Mayor, saying that the cathedral must be saved at all costs. This led to the formation of the St Paul's Watch, a large group of volunteers who sat up night after night ready to sweep off or cover with sand any incendiary devices that landed on or near the cathedral, so that they would not be followed by the force of the main attack. The St Paul's Watch was comprised of men and women from all walks of life and occupations; the poet John Betjeman was among them. It was largely due to their bravery that the cathedral remained intact.

During the war the cathedral bells remained silent, and only rang again on 24 August 1944 when Paris was liberated. The following year, on VE Day, St Paul's became a magnet for those wanting to celebrate the end of the war and 35,000 people gathered on the steps of the cathedral where ten impromptu services were held.

Sir Winston Churchill and his daughter Sarah on the steps of St Paul's Cathedral.

THE QUIRE

A view of the quire of St Paul's Cathedral, which was opened on 2 December 1697 for a thanksgiving service, 14 years before the cathedral was fully completed.

THE DOME

*On the inside of the dome are paintings by Sir James Thornhill. Above is the Whispering Gallery, then the Stone Gallery
with its views over the City; higher still is the Golden Gallery at the top of the dome, and finally the Golden Ball.*

THE CITY OF LONDON

Starting from Temple Bar in the west to the Tower of London in the east, the 677 acres of the City of London are governed by the Lord Mayor through the Corporation of London. Also known as the Square Mile, the City is no longer enclosed by a stone wall, but is in many ways separated from the rest of London by its unique customs and traditions. The City is the financial heart of the country.

A Brief History

Pre-Roman London
There is evidence of a settlement on the site of the City before the Romans arrived, but little is known about its origins.

43–50 A.D.
Aulus Plautius was ruler of Britain under the Roman Emperor Claudius, and, between 43 and 50, the Romans established a settlement which they called Londinium. It was a sophisticated and well ordered community; central heating, for example, which they had, was not reintroduced in Britain until the 19th century. Tacitus, writing in 67 A.D., refers to London as a flourishing trading city.

410
The Roman legions withdrew in 410, after which little is known about the history of the City until it was occupied by the Saxons in the 6th century.

604
King Ethelbert founded St Paul's Cathedral and is said to have had a palace in Aldermanbury, which was used by subsequent kings until King Canute moved to Westminster in about 1035.

1067
William the Conqueror granted the City a charter confirming the rights which they had enjoyed under Edward the Confessor. However, he did build the Tower of London to warn them not to step out of line.

12th century
Henry I granted the citizens of London the right to appoint their own sheriff.

1215
King John confirmed the right of the citizens to elect their own mayor and corporation, provided that each mayor was ratified by him or his officials.

Middle Ages
In medieval times, the city livery companies evolved, and eventually came to represent the citizens in their choice of mayor.

1547–
Henry VIII died, leaving the country with a debased currency, roaring inflation and mass unemployment. Sir Thomas Gresham eventually restored the currency and built the Royal Exchange as a meeting place for City merchants. They began an export drive which led to the foundation of great trading companies, including the East India Company, and to the establishment of the City of London as a centre of world commerce.

1665
The Great Plague which raged through the City was brought to London by the Norwegian brown rat, which arrived in the trading ships.

1666
The Fire of London started in September 1666, after a dry summer. It burned for five days and destroyed two thirds of the City, including the Royal Exchange and St Paul's Cathedral. Out of the disaster, Charles II saw the chance to create a totally new, stone-built metropolis. Within weeks of the fire, Christopher Wren had drawn up plans which included ordered streets, of three different widths, radiating from a central civic centre (a new Royal Exchange), and embankments along the river.

However, because the City relied on commerce for its survival, time was of the essence, and Londoners began rebuilding on the sites of their old homes. Various new designs were rejected and the City was eventually rebuilt on the old street plan. The commission for rebuilding London did, nevertheless, succeed in introducing building regulations to prevent such a disaster from happening again, and the new buildings were of brick and stone rather than timber-frame.

18th century
The 18th century saw the construction of many new buildings in the City, including the Bank of England, a new East India House, Ironmongers' Hall and the Mansion House.

19th century
The 19th century saw further expansion in the City, including the building of the General Post Office and the Prudential Assurance Building. London as a whole saw the opening of new educational establishments, a new sewage system (which helped to combat outbreaks of cholera), the Metropolitan Railway (London's first underground line) in 1863, the establishment of four main line stations, the first deep 'tube' line, and the foundation of the London General Omnibus Company.

20th century
The greatest alterations to the City skyline in the 20th century were caused by the Blitz in the Second World War and the office building boom in the 1980s.

Only about 5,800 people now live in the City of London, despite the fact that the workforce numbers some 360,000, three-quarters of whom are office workers.

THE CORPORATION OF LONDON

The Corporation of London is the governing body of the City, with the Lord Mayor at its head and the Guildhall as its home. The Corporation has Saxon roots and a constitution which developed out of the ancient Court of Hustings – the supreme court in the Middle Ages.

The Corporation is older than Parliament, and its authority stems from ancient privileges granted by the Crown and ratified by King John's Charters of 1199 and 1215. It has remained independent and non party-political, and is run by elected members known as the Court of Aldermen and the Court of Common Council. Until the 18th century, the Court of Aldermen was responsible for the government of the City, but gradually the day-to-day administrative work was taken over by the Court of Common Council, while the aldermanic body developed into what was effectively an Upper House.

William I was wise enough to realise that he should acknowledge this authority and he officially recognised the Corporation in 1067. It is said that he vanquished the entire country except for the City, and local legend has it that he is never referred to as 'the Conqueror' here. However, William did build the Tower of London just outside the City's east wall to keep an eye on its inhabitants.

As the City was the major source of financial loans to successive monarchs, the Corporation remained influential and was seen as so successful that it became the role model for Parliament at Westminster. In 1837, the Municipal Corporations Commission reported that the Corporation of London was the only one in the country not in need of reform.

THE CITY OF LONDON
A view of the City taken from St Paul's Cathedral.

A CLOSER LOOK

GUILDHALL

For over 800 years the Guildhall has been the home of the Corporation of London, and is the oldest centre of government in the country. The word 'guildhall' is said to derive from the Anglo-Saxon 'gild', meaning payment; the hall was probably the place where citizens would pay their taxes. The earliest reference to a London guildhall is 1128, and there is evidence of a guildhall on the current site from the mid-13th century, where the ancient Court of Hustings would meet. The present Guildhall was built between 1411 and 1430 and has twice survived catastrophic fires, the ancient walls emerging unscathed from both the Great Fire of 1666 and the Blitz in 1940.

As well as hosting the Lord Mayor's official banquets and being used for the entertainment of important visitors to the City, the Guildhall also has a much darker side. It was here that many state trials were held and traitors sentenced to death, the most famous victim being Lady Jane Grey.

Lady Jane Grey, the 'nine days queen', was the innocent victim of a scheme to further the family ambitions of the Lord Protector, John Dudley, Duke of Northumberland. Dudley persuaded the dying King Edward VI to name Lady Jane as his heiress presumptive, which the King did on 21 June 1553. Just one month before this, Dudley had arranged the marriage of Lady Jane to his teenage son, Lord Guilford, and the ceremony had taken place at Durham House in London on 21 May.

Jane was reluctant to accept the crown which her ambitious father-in-law forced upon her, but she was proclaimed Queen on 10 July 1553, after Edward VI's death had been made public (he died at Greenwich Palace on 6 July). However, the nobility were incensed by Dudley's presumption, and the people of England wanted Henry VIII's daughter Mary, not Jane, as their queen. Jane was deposed nine days later, on 19 July. Northumberland's plan had backfired and he was beheaded at Tower Hill on 22 August.

Lady Jane and Lord Guilford were both tried for treason at the Guildhall, convicted, and confined to the Tower under sentence of death. Mary I eventually agreed to their execution, and on 12 February 1554 Lady Jane bade farewell to her husband from her window as he walked to his death on Tower Hill. She herself was given the privilege of a more private execution on Tower Green later the same day.

Today, Guildhall is adorned with magnificent memorials to some of the nation's heroes, including Sir Winston Churchill, Nelson and the Duke of Wellington. The west gallery is guarded by the famous giants, Gog and Magog.

The giants Gog and Magog represent the legendary struggle between the ancient Britons and their Trojan invaders. The giants were originally named Gogmagog and Corineus, Corineus being the Trojan who defeated the British giant Gogmagog. By 1700, they were popularly known as Gog and Magog, titles which were later adopted officially. Legend has it that the Trojans, under the leadership of the Roman Brutus, were victorious, and in 1,000 B.C. founded the city of London as New Troy.

THE BANK OF ENGLAND

The origins of the Bank of England lie in the financing of a war. Towards the end of the 17th century, William III was running short of funds for the war against France. He had brought with him to England familiarity with a banking system which had been successfully running in his native Holland since the beginning of the 17th century, and he saw the establishment of a bank as a viable means of raising the necessary money.

Two City merchants (Michael Godfrey and a Scottish entrepreneur, William Paterson) proposed a scheme for a public loan in order to found a national bank which would lend its share capital to the government. The scheme was brought before parliament by Charles Montagu, and with his support the idea was successfuly approved in 1694. The Tunnage Act was passed to levy duties on shipping and alcohol, in order to guarantee an interest payment of 8% to subscribers of the loan, and for some time the Bank of England was known as the Tunnage Bank.

Advertisements invited the public to invest in the new bank. The response was overwhelming, and thousands of people queued to make deposits on the first day. In just eleven days, £1.2 million was raised by 1,268 people: the first entry in the deposit book was made by William and Mary, with a sum of £10,000. On 27 July 1694, the Bank of England was incorporated by royal charter, and England's first bank was officially open for business.

Before the establishment of the bank, money used in everyday life was tangible and existed only in the form of coins. These were produced by the Crown through the Treasury and stamped with the relevant monarch's head as a proof of authority. The advent of the bank introduced the idea of 'imaginary money' – promissory notes which represented deposits of gold coin or bullion held at the bank. Until 1931, when Britain came off the gold standard, these notes could be exchanged for gold; hence the words 'I promise to pay the bearer' on the face of each one. Today, bank notes are backed by securities instead of silver or gold.

THE BANK OF ENGLAND MUSEUM
Edward Wessex with gold bullion in the museum of the Bank of England.

The present Queen is the only monarch whose portrait has featured on a bank note. The monarch's head was introduced in 1960 as one of a number of measures intended to prevent forgeries. Forging bank notes is not a modern phenomenon: the first instance was in 1695, when Daniel Perrismore was fined and pilloried for forging 60 £100 notes. This led to the use of watermarked paper in 1697, and in the same year counterfeiting was made a felony punishable by death.

Another familiar symbol on our coinage and notes is the figure of Britannia, who is also the emblem for the Bank of England. The version of Britannia which we see today was drawn from life during the reign of Charles II. He was famous for wooing and winning mistresses, but he did not always have his way: Frances Stewart was particularly resistant to the King's advances and one of his more extreme forms of flattery was to have her depicted on the coins of the realm in her 'Minerva' costume. Even this failed to gain her affections. She turned instead to the 4th Duke of Richmond. Nevertheless, her image is used to this day as a depiction of Britannia.

The production of coins is not the responsibility of the Bank of England, but of the Royal Mint. The ancient Trial of the Pyx, a ritualised counting and testing of the previous year's coins, still takes place within the City. A form of monitoring such as this has been practised since Saxon times. Nowadays, the ceremony takes place at Goldsmith's Hall, one of the many livery company halls in the City.

The Queen's Remembrancer oversees the trial, for which a jury of eminent businessmen is sworn in. The jurors sit with two bowls in front of them, one of copper and one of wood. Coins selected for testing are put into the copper bowl and those not into the wooden one. Those to be tested are sent off for analysis, and eight weeks later the jury reconvenes to hear the results. The Trial of the Pyx is one of the ancient traditions which play a part in maintaining the strong links between the Bank and the merchants within the City.

THE BANK OF
ENGLAND MUSEUM

THE BANK OF ENGLAND
The Court Room, the Bank's equivalent of a board room.

THE LORD MAYOR OF LONDON

The Lord Mayor is the head of the Corporation of London, its chief magistrate, and the chairman of its two governing bodies, the Court of Aldermen and the Court of Common Council. The first recorded Lord Mayor was Henry Fitz-Ailwyn, who was appointed by the King's representative in the City, the Sheriff. The exact date of the start of his mayoralty is uncertain but the first reference to the post comes in 1189. Fitz-Ailwyn remained in office for another 23 years, until his death in 1212.

King John granted a charter in 1215 which gave the City the right to elect its own Sheriff and Lord Mayor, instead of the appointment being made by the monarch. The importance of the Lord Mayor was confirmed later the same year, when he was the only man who was not a baron to be elected to oversee the implementation of the Magna Carta.

Within the City of London, the Lord Mayor ranks second only to the sovereign, and if the sovereign wishes to enter the City on State occasions, permission must be granted. This permission takes the form of a ritual at Temple Bar, the boundary marking the ceremonial frontier between the City and Westminster: the Lord Mayor hands the monarch a pearl sword, pointing downwards; the monarch returns the sword and the Lord Mayor walks in procession before the sovereign, with the sword held upright.

The Lord Mayor is elected each Michaelmas Day, 29 September, by the Common Hall which is the body of liverymen. To be eligible, a candidate must have served as a sheriff and be an alderman. Common Hall selects two candidates from those put forward, and the Court of Aldermen makes the final choice.

The Lord Mayor's Show is rooted in the charter of 1215, in which King John stated that the new mayor must be presented to the sovereign or his justices in order for him to swear allegiance to the Crown. It is also an opportunity for him to be shown to the citizens of London. Elaborate pageants were common as early as the 14th century, and by the 15th these included the highly decorated barges of the livery companies, which gave rise to the use of the word 'float' for today's carnival vehicles.

The status of the Lord Mayor is reflected in many small details such as sharing with the monarch the secret password to the Tower of London, and in much grander statements such as his official residence, the palatial Mansion House. Before it was first occupied, in 1752, the Lord Mayor used his own house or the livery halls for entertaining. After the Great Fire in 1666, it was suggested that an official home should be built to reflect the increasing power and influence of the mayor.

THE LORD MAYOR'S COACH

The coach was custom made for the Lord Mayor in 1757, before which a coach had to be hired.

THE LORD MAYOR'S COACH

*The painted panels
are attributed to Cipriani and
Catton. Catton was a founder
member of the Royal Academy
and coachpainter to George III.*

FACT, FICTION AND FABLE

Dick Whittington

The most famous Lord Mayor of London was Richard Whittington, who in reality bore little relation to the fabled character who rose from rags to riches with the help of his trusted cat. The Dick Whittington of folklore reputedly heard the Bow Bells chiming 'turn again Whittington, thrice Lord Mayor of London': however, the earliest reference to this well-known story is a play entitled *The History of Richard Whittington*, which was published in 1605, nearly 200 years after his death.

The Whittington Stone stands on Highgate Hill to mark the spot where he supposedly heard the bells chime. It is inscribed:

> *Whittington Stone*
> *Sir Richard Whittington*
> *Thrice Lord Mayor of London*
> *1397 Richard II*
> *1406 Henry IV*
> *1420 Henry V*
> *Sheriff in 1393.*

The stone records two errors: Whittington was never knighted, and he was four times Lord Mayor. The real Richard Whittington lived in the late 14th/early 15th century, and was the son of a landowner from Gloucestershire. Shortly after his father's death he enrolled as an apprentice at the Mercers' Company and became a highly skilled tradesman. By the time he was 40 he had made a substantial fortune and in 1397 he was made Lord Mayor for the first time.

By 1397, Whittington was the City's richest merchant. He became an important banker to three successive kings but he was also a man with a social conscience: he spent great sums of money on building a library at Greyfriars, several new churches, a refuge for unmarried mothers at St Thomas's Hospital, and on improvements to Newgate Goal. Money left in his will also established colleges and almshouses which are still in operation nearly 600 years after his death. Perhaps his most unusual project, though, was to build a unique 128-seat public lavatory which was flushed by the Thames!

Another of the legacies left by Whittington was the library at Guildhall, which survived until the mid-16th century, when all the books were removed to furnish the library of the Lord Protector, Edward, Duke of Somerset.

LIVERY COMPANIES

There are 97 livery companies in the City, and places such as Milk Street, Ironmonger Lane, Poultry and Cloth Fair still mark the sites where these companies began. Livery companies have their origins in the medieval religious fraternities and trade guilds, when merchants would band together to promote their interests and look after their own. Craft guilds were established for the different trades from the 12th century, and fulfilled a wide variety of functions, not least of which was ensuring fair value: the guild organised apprenticeships, dictated who could work in its trade or craft, controlled prices, wages, working conditions, and looked after the welfare of its workers. The guild also carried out vigorous quality control, with regular inspections and severe punishments for poor workmanship. Later, guilds often amalgamated to form larger companies, often with liveries. Liverymen were the employers; yeomen the (free) workers.

The Weavers' Company was the first to gain a royal charter, in 1155, and others soon followed. In 1515, a list of livery companies was drawn up, with the most prestigious making up the 'Great Twelve'. The Mercers' Company was top of the list at no.1, and there was much squabbling about the order in which the others should be placed.

The Merchant Taylors and the Skinners could not determine which should take precedence, so it was decided that each year they would alternate between the sixth and seventh position, a practice which continues to this day. This is probably the origin of the expression 'at sixes and sevens'. Another common expression stems from the fact that poor workmanship would result in a member of a guild being publicly humiliated, fined or cast out: if this happened, the craftsman would not be allowed to work within the City walls, and would be 'sent to Coventry' or to the next available place where free craftsmen could operate.

VINTNERS' PROCESSION

Members of the Vintners parading through the streets on their election day – some are carrying posies which were traditionally used to combat the smell of the London streets.

In order to become a freeman, a member had to complete a seven-year apprenticeship with a master of their guild. Only then were they entitled to trade within the walls of the City; this was a means of keeping tight control over market forces, and the monopoly led to enormous wealth for the early livery companies. The Fishmongers' was one such company, which had complete monopoly of the selling of fish within the City. The fourth of the 'Great Twelve', it is one of the most ancient of the City guilds, with an unbroken history of 700 years. It was known to exist long before their official charter was granted to them by Edward I in 1272.

The present Fishmongers' Hall – the fourth to have stood on the site since the first hall was built in the early 1400s – stands where the 13th-century fishmongers first set up shop along the Thames.

One particular member of the Fishmongers' Company goes down in history for supposedly 'saving' the City. In 1381, the Prime Warden of the company was Sir William Walworth, at which time Wat Tyler was leading the Peasants' Revolt against the young King, Richard II. When the rebels reached London, Walworth met them face to face in the presence of the King. In the rowdy confusion, Walworth felt that the King's life was being threatened: he took matters into his own hands and stabbed Tyler, who later died from his injuries. The dagger is still preserved in the Fishmongers' Hall.

Like many other guilds, the Fishmongers' have members of the royal family in senior positions in the company, either as Prime Wardens or Masters. The present Duke of Edinburgh, Prince Philip, is a past Prime Warden and is still a member of the Court of Assistants for the company. In the hall are two of the most famous portraits of the present Queen and the Duke of Edinburgh, both painted by Annigoni.

One of the most colourful events of the year for the livery companies is the United Guild Service held at St Paul's in the spring. Members of the guilds fill the City's cathedral to capacity, and the occasion is one of very few opportunities to see livery men and women in all their finery. Religious worship has always been central to the guilds, and each has a patron saint and a strong link with a church or monastery.

SIR WILLIAM WALWORTH
Edward Wessex by the statue of Sir William Walworth in the Fishmongers' Hall. During the Peasants' Revolt in 1381 Sir William, who was then Prime Warden of the Fishmongers' Company, killed the leader of the rebels.

A CLOSER LOOK

THE COLLEGE OF ARMS

The College of Arms is the oldest college of its kind in the world and is home to the Royal Heralds, who were incorporated into a college by royal charter under King Richard III in 1484. There are 13 Royal Heralds, under the direction of the Duke of Norfolk, as hereditary Earl Marshal; they are appointed by the monarch as members of the royal household with special responsibilities for matters armorial, genealogical and ceremonial.

Heralds were first mentioned at about the time of the First Crusade in 1095, and were part of the households of European rulers and aristocracy from the late 12th century. At this time, armies were provided by wealthy landowners, who paid for the soldiers and their equipment, and tournaments were held as a practice for war: necessary practice, since movement was extremely difficult in the bulky armour. The tournaments were organised by the heralds, who consequently became experts in ceremonial matters. Heralds also acted as messengers, diplomats and army staff officers. Part of their duty was to be able to identify commanders by the devices painted on their banners, shields and surcoats, because faces were completely obscured by the helmets, so as well as becoming superb organisers they were also expert in the identification of coat armour or 'coats of arms'.

The first known coat of arms was that of Geoffrey of Anjou in 1127. Since 1307, senior heralds at the college have been granting arms on behalf of the sovereign. Henry VIII decided that all gentry must register their arms and pay for the privilege, so he sent heralds out into the shires to make detailed notes of the arms and family lineage.

The magnificent library at the college holds records of arms and family pedigrees dating back to the 1480s, with earlier records kept elsewhere under lock and key. The records include the coats of arms of many great names in British history, all of whom have chosen unique symbols to represent their standing in society. Most of the coats of arms at the college are copies, but that of George III is the original: he did not pay for his coat of arms on completion, and therefore he was not presented with it.

Arms today are granted to people of eminence as well as to organisations and companies. A herald will oversee the process, which includes researching the requested design to make sure that it has not been used before. The drawing and calligraphy are highly skilled jobs and are undertaken by a small group of artists specifically trained in the field.

The organisational skills for which the heralds were so noted in their early history are still required today: heralds are responsible for organising many formal occasions, including coronations, state funerals and the State Opening of Parliament.

ROYAL EXCHANGE

The Royal Exchange was first mooted by Richard Gresham, an eminent 16th-century merchant who saw the need for a meeting place where merchants could conduct their business. Lombard Street was where they had traditionally met but it proved to be impractical due to the increasing numbers of merchants trading along the open street. Gresham was influenced by a meeting place for merchants, or *bourse*, which operated in Antwerp, and so he submitted designs for a similar building in London. He enlisted Henry VIII's help in finding a site for the project but the negotiations fell through.

The *bourse* had to wait until Gresham's son Thomas, who was ambassador to Europe and chief of the foreign intelligence service, took up where his father left off. Thomas Gresham devoted much of his vast wealth to seeing his father's vision of a *bourse* become a reality in the heart of the City. A site was found, bought and cleared, and Gresham laid the first brick on 7 June 1566. The completed building was topped with an enormous grasshopper, the symbol of the Gresham family, and was opened by Queen Elizabeth I. She stated that it 'be proclaimed The Royal Exchange, and so be called from henceforth and not otherwise'. This was a sentiment repeated by Queen Victoria when she opened the third *bourse* on the site 300 years later.

When four fifths of the City burnt down in the Great Fire in 1666, the Royal Exchange was part of the devastation. It was considered to be such an important building that when Sir Christopher Wren drew up plans for a new city, all roads radiated from a new Royal Exchange. Wren's grand scheme was never realised but the new Royal Exchange was rebuilt on the same site and continued to be used for its original purpose until 1939 when it closed for business.

Today, Tower 42 stands on the site of Thomas Gresham's house. When the Tower was completed in 1980 it was the tallest building in Europe, and it is perhaps fitting that such an extravagant symbol of financial prowess, with its spectacular views of the Square Mile, should be built upon the house of such a great figure of English commercial history.

THE ROYAL EXCHANGE

TOWER 42

Tower 42, formerly the National Westminster Tower, seen from St Paul's Cathedral. When the tower was completed in 1980 it was the tallest building in Europe, 52 storeys and 600 ft high.

PUDDING LANE

The Great Fire which devastated the City in 1666 started at Thomas Faryner's bakery in Pudding Lane. The lane is said to be named after animals' 'puddings' (the medieval word for guts and entrails, as in 'black pudding'), which were brought down Pudding Lane on the way from the butchers' shops at Eastcheap to the Thames dung barges.

ROYAL PALACES

There are several palaces in and around London, but the story of why the present sovereign lives at Buckingham Palace rather than any other can be traced back through just three palaces: St James's, Whitehall and Westminster. What these three palaces have in common is that they were each the principal home of the Court.

When the sovereign was the executive power in the country the Court was the collective name for the administration which supported the King or Queen and made everything happen. The Court still exists, albeit on a much smaller scale, and with many of its functions delegated to other bodies. Nonetheless, the administrative centre of the kingdom remains in this part of London. These three palaces were, in their time, the grandest and most important of the royal buildings; indeed, Westminster is still arguably the most important. The story of each one is steeped in power and majesty and tragedy – for they have each suffered a devastating fire.

BUCKINGHAM PALACE

The east façade, with the Victoria Memorial in the foreground. Buckingham Palace, the home of the current sovereign, has been part of the royal story for a surprisingly short time.
The first monarch to use the palace as an official residence was Queen Victoria in 1837.

WESTMINSTER ABBEY

A Brief History

2nd century
Legend has it that there was a Roman Temple to Apollo on Thorney Island, which was destroyed by an earthquake in the 2nd century. In its place, a native king, whose Roman name was Lucius, built the first church there.

7th century
The legend continues that the church of St Peter was rebuilt by King Sebert of the East Saxons, and that St Peter appeared in person to consecrate it.

10th century
The first historic account is that Archbishop (now Saint) Dunstan, under a charter from King Edgar, restored a church or minster on the site, which became known as Westminster. A monastery was probably established at about this time.

11th century
Dunstan's minster was laid waste by a Danish invasion and was again revived, this time by King Canute, c. 1035. Canute also built a palace at Westminster.

1044–65
Edward the Confessor added to Canute's palace and restored the monastery, dedicating it to St Peter. He demolished the old church and devoted 'a tenth of his entire substance' to building the abbey, which was consecrated in 1065.

1220–72
Very little remains of Edward the Confessor's abbey, and nothing of his palace. The abbey we see today was built about 150 years later by Henry III, who added a Lady Chapel (later replaced by Henry VII) in 1220, and in 1245 began rebuilding the abbey. He completed the Chapter House in 1259.

1272
Henry III died in 1272 before finishing work on the new abbey, which was not completed until after the reign of Henry VII, over 250 years later.

1503–32
Work went on in a rather piecemeal fashion until Henry VII's patronage. In 1503, he began his replacement Lady Chapel which was completed just before his death in 1509. Work continued under the supervision of the abbot, John Islip, who died in 1532, leaving the nave finished, and the west towers raised to roof level. The work begun in 1220 by Henry III was virtually completed.

1540
The monastery was dissolved but, because of its royal associations, not destroyed, and the abbey became the cathedral of Westminster.

1698–1723
The abbey had been mutilated by the Parliamentarians during the Civil War, and between 1698 and 1723 was extensively renovated by Sir Christopher Wren, whose work was continued by Nicholas Hawksmoor and completed by John James.

1827–71
A century after Wren, Edward Blore rearranged the quire, ignoring the need for urgent repairs to the Chapter House. These works were carried out later by Sir George Gilbert Scott.

Westminster, like the City of London, is a city in its own right. It gained its name from the minster built in the 10th century on the site of what is now Westminster Abbey, 'to the west of the old City of London'. From the 11th century, the precinct was for centuries to consist only of church, monastery and palace. The abbey is built on what was once a marshy island called Thorney Island, where the river Tyburn runs into the Thames, and its long association with royalty has given it a unique position in the country. Monarchs are crowned here and buried here, and services to mark historic occasions of national importance are held here.

EDWARD THE CONFESSOR

Edward had vowed to make a pilgrimage to the tomb of Saint Peter in Rome, but was dissuaded by his Great Council which feared disorder in his absence. Pope Leo IX agreed to release the King from his vow, on condition that he would found or restore a monastery to St Peter. Edward therefore moved his court to Westminster (also a sound political move), and began building an abbey, dedicated to St Peter, on the site of King Canute's church. Edward apportioned to the work 'a tenth of his entire substance in gold, silver, cattle and all other possessions'.

The new abbey church of St Peter was designed in the Norman style, a natural choice since Edward's mother was Norman and Edward had spent much of his early life in Normandy. The abbey at Westminster was the first cruciform church in England and was derived from the church at Jumièges in Normandy, the remains of which survive to this day.

By Christmas 1065 the abbey was far enough advanced to be consecrated, although the Bayeux Tapestry indicates that it may not have been completed until as late as 1080. On 27 December 1065 Edward withdrew to his deathbed, giving orders that the church should be consecrated the following day, Holy Innocent's Day. Eight days later he died and was buried before the high altar.

A magnificent tomb was constructed for Edward. Decorated in gold and resting on a Purbeck marble and mosaic base, it remains one of the greatest treasures of English history. It is also unique, being the only shrine in the

WESTMINSTER ABBEY
The West Front, which was the last part of the abbey to be completed. It was built by Sir Christopher Wren, who was Surveyor to the Abbey from 1698–1723, and was completed in 1745.

country which still contains the body of its saint.

After Edward's death, miracles were believed to have taken place (including his transfiguration and the curing of a blind bellringer and a hunchback), and when the tomb was opened in 1102 the body was found to be intact. King Edward was canonised by Pope Alexander III in 1161, and his shrine remains the most sacred place in the abbey.

WILLIAM THE CONQUEROR

Edward the Confessor left no heir. He allegedly promised the crown to William, Duke of Normandy, but on his deathbed is said to have named Harold Godwinsson, who was crowned Harold II on the day of Edward's burial.

There were several other claimants to the throne. One was Harold Hardrada of Norway, whom Harold II defeated at Stamford Bridge on 25 September 1066. Another was William, Duke of Normandy, who landed at Pevensey Bay in Sussex three days after the battle at Stamford Bridge, defeated Harold at the Battle of Hastings on 14 October, and was duly acknowledged king.

William was crowned at Westminster Abbey on Christmas Day 1066. He was presented to the people in both French and English, and they were called upon to acclaim him king, a French ritual which is integrated into the English coronation service to this day. In 1086, William ordered an inventory of his new kingdom: the Domesday Book.

William was the illegitimate son of Robert, Duke of Normandy and Herleve, a tanner's daughter, and was known in France as William the Bastard. In 1035, at the age of eight or nine (the exact date of his birth is unknown), he succeeded his father, who had no legitimate heir, as Duke of Normandy. His formal claim to the English throne was by inheritance: his wife, Matilda of Flanders, was directly descended from Alfred the Great, and William himself was first cousin once removed to Edward the Confessor, whom he visited in 1051, at which time Edward designated William as his successor. In practical terms, his claim was by conquest. William died in 1087 while campaigning in France, after the pommel of his saddle struck him in the stomach, causing fatal internal injuries.

William's coronation at Westminster Abbey began a tradition which has seen the coronation of 39 successive kings and queens at the abbey: every monarch thereafter, with the exception of Edward V and Edward VIII, neither of whom was crowned.

SHRINE OF EDWARD THE CONFESSOR

The shrine lies in the Chapel of St Edward the Confessor, surrounded by the tombs of Henry III, Edward I and Queen Eleanor of Castille, Edward III and Queen Philippa of Hainault, and Richard II and Queen Anne of Bohemia.

FACT, FICTION AND FABLE

St Peter at Westminster

The legendary account of King Sebert's church of St Peter, built on Thorney Island in the 7th century, tells that St Peter appeared in person to consecrate the church.

A fisherman, Edricus, was casting his nets on the Thames when he was beckoned by a figure on the southern shore. Slowly he rowed over, and the stranger asked for a passage to Thorney Island. During the crossing, his passenger told Edricus that he too was a fisherman and that he had come to dedicate the church that was to bear his name.

Edricus doubted the stranger's tale, but moored his boat and watched as the stranger stepped on to the shore. Suddenly everything was bathed in a heavenly light. When the stranger returned to the boat, he told Edricus to let down his nets for a catch; he did as he was instructed and was rewarded with a catch of prize salmon.

The monks of Westminster set great store by this tale and used to claim a tax of a tenth of all fish caught in the river near Thorney Island. A festival is held annually on 30 June in the abbot's public dining hall. Everyone is attired in ceremonial dress and a salmon is presented to the abbey by local fishmongers to mark St Peter's Day.

HENRY III

Henry III was crowned twice. The first time was at Gloucester Cathedral in 1216, when London was unsafe and the nine-year-old King's nobles were anxious to establish the legitimacy of his succession. The second coronation was at Westminster Abbey when King Henry was thirteen.

On 16 May 1220, the day before his second coronation, Henry laid the foundation stone of the Lady Chapel and so began his long association with Westminster Abbey.

Henry became obsessed with Edward the Confessor who, since his canonisation, had become a cult figure. He was determined to demonstrate his veneration for the saint by rebuilding the abbey to house a magnificent shrine 'for the deposition of the relics of the blessed Edward'.

On 6 July 1245 work began on demolishing and then rebuilding the abbey, a colossal task which nearly bankrupted the country and almost led to civil war. It was supervised in turn by three master masons: Henry de Reyns to 1253, Master John of Gloucester to 1260 and Master Robert of Beverley to 1285. The consecration of the Abbey was celebrated in 1269, although work continued up to Henry's death in 1272, and beyond: the abbey was described as fully finished to the end of the quire in 1285. However, Henry's intention had been to alter the western part of the building in keeping with his new work, and this would have to wait for the patronage of Henry VII.

Reigning monarchs governed with the aid of a Great Council, which during Henry's reign became known as parliament: the first Parliament of England was summoned to meet at Westminster on 28 January 1265, after Simon de Montfort had defeated Henry at the Battle of Lewes. Later the same year, Henry's son Edward (later Edward I) defeated de Montfort at Evesham and, with Henry growing senile, became the effective ruler.

Henry died in 1272 and was buried in Edward the Confessor's coffin, the saint having been moved to a grander one. Henry's heart, however, was taken to Fontevrault Abbey in France, to be buried with his Angevin ancestors.

FACT, FICTION AND FABLE

King Canute

It was at Westminster that King Canute (or Cnut), tried to stop the tide. According to John Norden, a 16th-century historian, Canute 'passed by the Thamys, which ran by that Pallace, at the flowing of the tide; and making staie neere the water, the waves cast some part of their water towards him. This Canutus conjured the waves by his regal commande to proceede no farther. The Thamas, unacquainted with this new god, held on its course, flowinge as of custome it used to do and refrained not to assayle him neere to the knees.'

There are two schools of thought about this tale. The popular story maintains that Canute was arrogant enough to believe that he had the powers of a god and was surprised when the tide did not obey him. The other version is that he was fed up with being revered as a god and said to his courtiers that he would prove he was not divine by showing them that the tide would not obey his command.

Whichever the reason, actions speak louder than words and Canute is remembered as the king who believed he could control the tide.

A CLOSER LOOK

CHAPTER HOUSE

The Chapter House at Westminster Abbey was built by Henry III, and was completed in 1253. It is the second largest Chapter House in England, after Lincoln. The Chapter House was an important administrative building: much of the business of the monastery was conducted here, senior guests were received, and superior members of the order buried.

The name Chapter House derives from the practice whereby the monks would gather after Mass to hear a chapter of the Benedictine Rule read aloud. The abbot or a delegate would then give a sermon and the day's business followed. Monastic discipline was also discussed at chapter meetings; any breaches of the Rule would be reported and often the offending monk would be beaten with a rod or a bundle of sticks. Benedictine Rule dictated that during this punishment 'all brethren should bow down with a kind and brotherly compassion'.

The Chapter House is also where early Parliament meetings were held. The first meeting of Henry III's Great Council took place here on 26 March 1257, and for 200 years, from the middle of the 14th century unti 1547, it was used for meetings of the House of Commons.

Since the Reformation, the Chapter House has belonged to the Crown, not the abbey, and was used as a record office until 1863. During this time the windows were blocked in, an internal gallery was built and the vault was destroyed; the Chapter House was restored to its former glory from 1866–72 by Sir George Gilbert Scott.

The octagonal room is 50 ft in diameter and the huge windows are each 39 ft high. Paintings on the walls include scenes of the Last Judgement and the Apocalypse. Sir George Gilbert Scott's restoration revealed possibly the best example in the country of a medieval encaustic tiled floor.

SOUTH TRANSEPT ROSE WINDOW

The tracery of the rose window was remodelled in 1849–50 by Sir George Gilbert Scott, who was appointed Surveyor of the Fabric in 1849. The glass was replaced in 1901 as a memorial to the 1st Duke of Westminster.

THE QUIRE
The quire and east end of Henry III's abbey, which was consecrated in 1269,
pictured during Evensong in 1996.

HENRY VII

Henry VII decided to build a new Lady Chapel at Westminster Abbey as a shrine to his uncle, Henry VI, who was deposed in 1461 and murdered in the Tower of London in 1471. After Henry VI, the Wars of the Roses brought Edward IV, Edward V and Richard III to the throne, before Henry VII defeated Richard III at the Battle of Bosworth and was crowned king.

Henry VI had been buried at Chertsey Abbey, where rumours of miracles began to circulate and a cult took root. The Yorkists moved Henry's body to Windsor in 1484 but the cult persisted. When Henry VII came to power, he resolved to turn this cult to his advantage by having Henry VI canonised and building a Lady Chapel as a shrine to the new royal saint. Pope Julius II agreed to the canonisation, but demanded such a large sum of money that the parsimonious Henry VII changed his mind, although he was not deflected from his plan to build a chapel in honour of the Virgin Mary.

The foundation stone of Henry VII's Lady Chapel was laid on 24 January 1503, and building was completed shortly before his death in 1509. Although originally conceived as a shrine to Henry VI, the chapel in fact became a monument to Henry VII, with a magnificent tomb by Torrigiano being erected in 1512.

The chapel is famous for its fan-vaulted ceiling, of which Washington Irving wrote: 'Stone seems, by the winning labour of the chisel, to have been robbed of its weight and density, suspended aloft as if by magic, and the fretted roof achieved with the wonderful minuteness and airy security of a cobweb.'

After Henry VII's death, it was left to John Islip, the Abbot, to complete the work begun over 250 years earlier by Henry III.

A CLOSER LOOK

THE JERUSALEM CHAMBER

On 20 March 1413, St Cuthbert's Day, Henry IV stopped at Westminster Abbey to pray at the shrine of St Edward on his way to the Holy Land, where he intended to visit the Holy Sepulchre in Jerusalem.

It had been predicted that Henry would die in Jerusalem, but while in the abbey he was suddenly taken ill with apoplexy. As he lay dying, he asked where he was, and was told that he had been carried to the Jerusalem Chamber in the Abbot's House. He replied: 'Now I know I shall die in this chamber, according to the prophecy of me beforehand, that I should die in Jerusalem.'

On the painted oak ceiling of the Jerusalem Chamber (left), the mitre and initials of the abbot Nicholas Litlyngton alternate with the crown and initials of Richard II.

CHAPEL OF THE PYX

In the East Cloister of the abbey are the vaulted Chapel of the Pyx and the abbey museum. The two rooms were once joined, and are the oldest remaining part of the abbey, dating from the late 11th century. Originally a chapel, the room was used from the 14th century as the treasure house of the monastery and to safeguard the Pyx: a large chest containing standard samples of the coinage of the realm.

The huge oak door of the chamber has six locks, each with a separate key. Each key was in the safekeeping of a different person, and in order to open the door, all six keyholders had to attend. A stone sill in the cloister allows the door to open only enough for one person to enter at a time.

HENRY VII'S LADY CHAPEL

Miraculum orbis – *a wonder of the world – was how Henry VII's Lady Chapel was described*
by contemporary historian John Leland.
Above: *The exterior of the chapel from Victoria Tower.*
Right: *The fan-vaulted ceiling, 'suspended aloft as if by magic...with the airy security of a cobweb'.*

THE PALACE OF WESTMINSTER

A Brief History

c. 1035
The first palace at Westminster was built by King Canute.

1044–65
Edward the Confessor added to Canute's palace.

1097
William Rufus (son of William the Conqueror) built the vast and impressive Westminster Hall in 1097 as an extension to the palace. Nothing else remains of the early palace.

Westminster Hall became the centre of the administrative life of the royal court. Grand Councils and some early parliaments were held in the hall, and from the 13th century until 1882 it housed the Law Courts.

1512
In 1512 the palace was damaged by fire, and Henry VIII abandoned Westminster, first sharing Lambeth Palace with the Archbishop of Canterbury and later moving to Whitehall Palace.

The Palace of Westminster remained the administrative centre of the kingdom.

1547–
Under Edward VI, the Palace of Westminster became used as a home for both Houses of Parliament.

1834–52
The greater part of the Palace of Westminster was destroyed in a fire, leaving only Westminster Hall, the crypt of St Stephen's Chapel and part of the cloisters intact.

Sir Charles Barry won the competition to design new buildings specifically for the two Houses of Parliament, and Augustus Pugin was responsible for the interiors. The two Houses settled permanently into their new homes at the opening of the 1852 session of Parliament.

10 May 1941
The Palace of Westminster had already been damaged eleven times by bombs. On 10 May incendiary and high explosive bombs fell in such numbers on the House of Commons that the entire building was set ablaze.

1945–50
Sir Giles Gilbert Scott was commissioned to rebuild the Chamber of the House of Commons.

For nearly 500 years, from the time of King Canute to the reign of Henry VIII, the Palace of Westminster was the official residence of the reigning monarch and his court. In an age when the government carries more administrative power than the monarch, Westminster Palace retains its prominence as the Houses of Parliament.

THE EVOLUTION OF PARLIAMENT

The word 'parliament' means an assembly or council, and originally referred to the King's Councils of bishops, nobles and ministers gathered at the behest of the monarch. The King would sit on his throne and announce, 'I have summoned you here because . . .'; a tradition which is continued at the State Opening of Parliament, although the monarch now speaks with the words of his or her Prime Minister's Cabinet.

The two houses of Parliament, the Lords and the Commons, evolved over many centuries. The inclusion of representatives from local communities was introduced by Henry III and Simon de Montfort in 1265, after which it became increasingly common for monarchs to summon representatives or 'knights' from the shires and 'burgesses' from the towns. The name Commons, by which the house of burgesses was known, did not signify common people; it referred to the local communities which the House of Commons still represents.

These two groups did not meet separately until 1332. After this time, both Houses would meet in the presence of the King, usually in the Painted Chamber (where the State Opening of Parliament continues to take place today), and then the Lords would retire to the White Chamber and the Commons to wherever they could find room; usually in the Chapter House or the refectory of Westminster Abbey. As Parliament grew in size, this became less

convenient and Edward VI agreed to allow the abandoned Palace of Westminster to become a permanent home for the Commons. Although it has officially remained a royal palace, this move helped to establish the separation of crown and government.

The House of Lords continued to meet in the White Chamber and later moved to the White Hall, and by 1550 the deconsecrated royal chapel of St Stephen had become the permanent home of the House of Commons.

It was in the cellars beneath the White Hall that the Gunpowder Plot was foiled. Acting on the orders of the Privy Council, which had received an anonymous warning, the Earl of Suffolk searched the cellars on the night of 4 November 1605 and discovered Guy Fawkes hiding there with 36 barrels of gunpowder and a slow fuse. The Plotters intended to blow up both Houses along with King James I, who was due to open Parliament the following day. Nearly four hundred years later, the cellars are still searched by the Yeomen of the Guard before each State Opening of Parliament.

At the start of each Sitting Day in the House of Commons, the Speaker enters the chamber, preceded by the Sergeant at Arms who carries the mace. Parliament is not properly consituted if the mace is not present. The mace is derived from a medieval close-quarter battle weapon, originally used for the protection of the sovereign, which became accepted worldwide as a symbol of office. Ceremonially, it represents the power delegated by the ruler to the bearer of the mace.

THE PALACE OF WESTMINSTER

Looking across the Thames at one of London's most famous landmarks, the Houses of Parliament, with Victoria Tower
to the left and the Clock Tower (better known as Big Ben) to the right. The Palace of Westminster has been home
to the Houses of Parliament since the reign of Edward VI.

A CLOSER LOOK

WESTMINSTER HALL

Westminster Hall was built in 1097 by William Rufus, son of William the Conqueror. It was the largest hall in the kingdom but Rufus protested that it was 'a mere bedchamber compared with what I had intended to build'. The hall is now the vestibule of the House of Commons, having been retained by Sir Charles Barry in his design for the Palace of Westminster. It is connected to the rest of the palace by St Stephen's Hall.

The oak hammerbeam roof (below) dates from the reign of Richard II and is acknowledged as the finest medieval timber roof in northern Europe. It has the widest unsupported ceiling span in the country.

The hall has witnessed many pivotal moments of British history. Since 1099, it has seen coronation celebrations, the lying-in-state of monarchs and statesmen, the installation of Oliver Cromwell as Lord Protector and the trial of Charles I.

THE PALACE OF WESTMINSTER
A view of Victoria Tower and the Thames from the Clock Tower (Big Ben).

A VIEW
of
THE TRIAL OF THE KING

THE TRIAL OF CHARLES I

In January 1642, Charles I burst into the former royal chapel of St Stephen's, where the House of Commons was sitting, and demanded the arrest of five members on charges of treason against him. When the King asked where the five members were, the Speaker, William Lenthall, replied, 'I have neither eyes to see, nor tongue to speak in this place, but as this House is pleased to direct me.' The King had no choice but to withdraw, and since then no monarch has set foot in the Commons chamber.

Seven years later, the tables were turned and Charles found himself brought to trial by Parliament for treason against the state. His autocratic behaviour towards Parliament had led to the Civil War in which Oliver Cromwell's New Model Army had defeated the royalists. The trial took place in Westminster Hall in January 1649 and lasted for seven days. Charles's judges were commissioners appointed by the Commons but Charles refused to accept the authority of the court, keeping his hat on throughout the proceedings. One woman was branded with hot irons for shouting out her support for the King, and others were silenced by having muskets trained on them.

Charles I was found guilty of high treason and condemned to death by execution. His death warrant was signed by, among others, Oliver Cromwell. The date for his execution was set for 30 January, and would take place on a scaffold in front of the Banqueting House at Whitehall Palace.

THE TRIAL OF CHARLES I
The King kept his hat on throughout the proceedings, refusing to accept the authority of the court.

A CLOSER LOOK

ST STEPHEN'S CHAPEL

The original St Stephen's Chapel, the royal chapel of the Palace of Westminster, was destroyed by fire. It was rebuilt by Edward I and finished by Edward III in 1347. The King worshipped in the chapel and the courtiers in the crypt. The chapel was secularised at the Reformation, under the Chantries Act of 1547, and by 1550 had become the home of the House of Commons.

St Stephen's was perfect for use as a debating chamber. Members sat in the choir stalls on the north and south walls, and the Speaker's chair was placed where the altar had been. The mace was placed on a table where the lectern had been.

Of St Stephen's Chapel, only the crypt, St Mary Undercroft, survived the fire of 1834, and this was restored by Edward M. Barry (son of Sir Charles Barry) in the 1860s as a chapel for members of both Houses of Parliament.

A CLOSER LOOK

BIG BEN

The Clock Tower at Westminster is known as 'Big Ben', although the name actually refers to the huge bell which chimes the hour. It is thought to be named after Sir Benjamin Hall, Chief Commissioner of Works at the time it was made. Barry's new Houses of Parliament were finished by 1852, but the Clock Tower was not completed until 1858, with the clock and bell becoming operational on 31 May 1859.

The clock was the subject of much controversy and was eventually made by E.J. Dent to a design by Edmund Beckett Denison, against the wishes of Charles Barry, who preferred Benjamin Vulliamy, the Queen's clockmaker. Dent had to meet very stringent requirements for accuracy: the first stroke of each hour must be correct to within one second, and the clock's performance was to be checked twice a day at the Greenwich Observatory by telegraph.

The original bell was cast in Stockton-on-Tees using a mixture of metals specified by Denison but which the bellfounders felt was unsuitable. The 16-ton bell was brought to London by sea and river, and tested for tone before it was hung in the tower: during the tests, Denison increased the size of the clapper from 7 cwt to 13 cwt, which caused a 4 ft crack in the bell.

Big Ben was recast by George Mears at London's oldest factory, the Whitechapel Bell Foundry. Mears stipulated that the bell should be struck by a hammer of no more than 4 cwt but when the bell cracked within a few months it was discovered that Denison had fitted a 7 cwt hammer. The clapper was modified and the bell still chimes to this day, complete with crack.

There were also problems with the hands of the clock. The original 2.5-ton cast-iron hands were too heavy for the mechanism to move them, so they were replaced by lighter gunmetal hands. The minute hands fell several feet every time they passed the vertical, so they too were replaced, this time by hollow copper hands, although the gunmetal hour hands remain.

Part way up the Clock Tower is a cell known as the Number One Room, in which agitators or members of either House could be locked up. The last time a Member of Parliament was locked in the Number One Room was in 1880. The last person to be confined there, in 1902, was Emmeline Pankhurst, the leader of the suffragette movement.

THE FIRE OF 1834

Until it was abolished in 1826, the Court of the Exchequer had used notched tally sticks as a record of accounts due. In 1834 it was decided to burn them in a furnace under the Lords' Chamber in the old Palace of Westminster. The heat became so intense that by the following morning most of the Palace of Westminster lay in smoking ruins; the spectacle had been such that the army had been called out to control the crowds in order to allow the firemen to fight the blaze.

Charles Dickens spoke scathingly on the subject: 'The sticks were housed at Westminster, and it would naturally occcur to any intelligent person that nothing could be easier than to allow them to be carried away for firewood by the miserable people who live in that neighbourhood. However, they never had been useful, and official routine required that they never should be, and so the order went forth that they should be privately and confidentially burned.'

The fire was actually a blessing in disguise; Edward the Confessor's old palace was unsuitable for the machinery of government by Parliament, and its destruction provided an opportunity to design purpose-built accommodation. Sir Charles Barry won the competition to design the new Houses of Parliament, selecting a Perpendicular Gothic style in keeping with Westminster Abbey. He commissioned Augustus Pugin to work on the interior of the new palace; as well as nearly all the internal detail, Pugin also designed the close Perpendicular detail for Barry. The two Houses were in their new homes for the opening of the 1852 session of parliament.

THE PALACE OF WESTMINSTER
Victoria Tower from Victoria Tower Gardens.
Built between 1835 and 1860 by Sir Charles Barry and Augustus Pugin.

FACT, FICTION AND FABLE

Sir Charles Barry

Born in 1795, between 1817 and 1820 Barry travelled through France, Italy, Greece, Turkey, Egypt and Palestine, studying buildings and making sketches. In 1823 he won the competition to design St Peter's, Brighton, and then designed several 'pre-archaeological' Gothic churches.

Barry also designed the Royal Institution of Fine Arts, Manchester; the Manchester Athenaeum; and the Traveller's Club and the Reform Club in London, as well as the new Palace of Westminster which was completed by his son, Edward M. Barry. Charles Barry died in 1860.

Augustus Welby Northmore Pugin

Pugin was born in London in 1812, the son of a French architectural draughtsman, Auguste Pugin, who worked in the office of John Nash. Augustus Pugin initially helped his father edit books on Gothic architecture but soon received commissions of his own: before he was twenty he was designing furniture for Windsor Castle and stage sets for the theatre.

Pugin showed a religious passion for the Gothic, and his biography reads like the plot of a Gothic novel: shipwrecked in 1830, married in 1831, lost his wife in 1832, married again in 1833, lost his second wife in 1844, married again in 1849, lost his mind in 1851 and died in Bedlam mental hospital in 1852.

In his work with Barry on the Houses of Parliament, Pugin's obsession with the detail of Gothicism extended to coat hooks and ink wells, and he even asked for his meals to be laid out in Gothic style. Pugin designed Cheadle church in Staffordshire, Nottingham Cathedral, and St Augustine's, Ramsgate, which he paid for himself and which stands next to his own house.

WHITEHALL PALACE

A Brief History

1514
Thomas Wolsey became Archbishop of York in 1514. The official residence that he acquired had been rebuilt in the 15th century but Wolsey began to extend the house and grounds on a lavish scale. He renamed the house York Place.

1528
In 1528 Wolsey built a Great Hall at York Place, where he entertained Henry VIII and his court in a spectacularly lavish manner. The Cardinal was also renowned for his wines, and his wine cellar, originally under the Guard Room and now resited deep underneath the Ministry of Defence, is one of the few parts of Whitehall Palace to survive.

1529
The desirability of York Place had not been lost on Henry who, since 1512, when fire had damaged Westminster Palace, had been sharing the Archbishop of Canterbury's residence at Lambeth. When Wolsey fell from favour in 1529, Henry appropriated York Place for the Crown, and decided to make it his principal residence. The name was again changed, this time to Whitehall Palace. The name may refer to the light stone used in some of the new building work, but it is more likely that it derives from 'White Hall', the term used at the time for any grand hall where festivities took place.

Shakespeare refers to the name change in *Henry VIII* (Act IV, scene 1):

*You must no more call it York Place,
that's past:
For since the Cardinal fell, that title's lost;
'Tis now the King's and call'd Whitehall.*

1529–47
Henry, too, carried out an extensive rebuilding programme, transforming Whitehall Palace into the largest palace in Europe. It covered 23 acres and stretched most of the length of modern Whitehall, from St James's Park to the west, to the Thames to the east. It was a rambling agglomeration of buildings containing over 1,000 apartments.

1547
By the time Henry died in 1547 he had built a palace in which the King's public and private accommodation was combined but the royal apartments were separated from the financial and legal machinery of the Crown, which remained at Westminster. He had also laid out gardens and orchards, built real tennis courts, a cockpit and a tiltyard, and had enclosed Hyde Park as a hunting park. The court nevertheless continued to move frequently between the 60 palaces that Henry owned.

1558–1603
During the reign of Elizabeth, the Great Hall of Whitehall Palace was much used for dramatic performances, but the rest of the vast palace was allowed to run down.

1603–
The Stuart kings restored Whitehall Palace to importance as the main seat of the court. James I employed Inigo Jones and John Webb to draw up plans for an enormous new palace, but only the Banqueting House was ever built. It is the only part of Whitehall Palace which remains today, other than Wolsey's wine cellar.

1698
On 2 January 1698 the diarist John Evelyn wrote: 'Whitehall burnt; nothing but walls and ruins left.' The previous day, a Dutch maid, one of hundreds of Netherlanders who had accompanied William and Mary to London, was drying her linen over a charcoal brazier in a wood-panelled room. Fire soon raged through the palace and, with the Thames frozen over, the firefighters were unable to find enough water to put it out.

Before Whitehall was appropriated as a royal palace by Henry VIII in 1529, the building was the official residence of the Archbishop of York and was known as York House.

BANQUETING HOUSE

In January 1619, two workmen were clearing up after Twelfth Night celebrations in James I's Banqueting House at Whitehall Palace, and decided to dispose of the rubbish by setting fire to it. There had been two earlier Banqueting Houses on the site: a temporary structure of wood and canvas, built in 1572, and a similar structure built by Queen Elizabeth I in 1581, but richly painted and with glass windows. James I pulled this down in 1606, and erected a permanent building which he never liked but which opened in 1608. Now, eleven years later, it was destroyed.

Inigo Jones was commissioned to build yet another Banqueting House, which was begun in 1619. Classically formal in the Palladian style, it was the first purely Renaissance building to be built in London, and is widely acknowledged not only as a masterpiece of Jones's work, but as 'one of the finest rooms in the country'. It still stands today.

Inigo Jones introduced the Palladian style to England, after studying the buildings and theoretical writings of the Italian Andrea Palladio. He also, as a stage designer, brought back Italian expertise in the fields of scenery and stage machinery. The new Banqueting House, on the same site as the earlier one, took three years to build and was finished in 1622. It had two storeys and a basement which was used to store the stage machinery used for the elaborate masques which were performed there.

In 1630 Charles I commissioned Rubens to paint the nine ceiling panels, lavishly framed in curlicued gold, which were completed in 1634. The panels are allegories of greatness, goodness, wisdom, the victories of the Stuarts and the unification of England and Scotland. Rubens received a knighthood for his work.

Charles I was a lover of art and collected over 460 paintings at Whitehall, including 28 Titians, nine Raphaels and several Van Dycks. Most of this collection was dispersed during the Commonwealth when Oliver Cromwell lived in Whitehall as Lord Protector. It was from the Banqueting House that Charles I walked to the scaffold.

After the fire of 1698 which destroyed the rest of the palace, the Banqueting House was converted by Sir Christopher Wren into a Chapel Royal. In 1809, it became the Chapel of the Horse Guards, was restored in 1829 and again used as a Chapel Royal until 1890 when it became a museum. In 1963, it was restored and redecorated and opened to the public. Its modern appearance dates from the early 19th century when it was refaced in Portland stone.

BANQUETING HOUSE
All that remains of Whitehall Palace is the Banqueting House,
built for James I by Inigo Jones from 1619–22.

CARDINAL WOLSEY

Cardinal Thomas Wolsey dominated the political and ecclesiastical life of England during the early part of Henry VIII's reign. Historians still argue about whether he or Henry VIII was really running the country until 1529, when Wolsey fell out of favour and was removed from office.

Reputedly the son of an Ipswich butcher, Wolsey was educated at Oxford and became a fellow of Magdalen College in 1497. He left to serve as chaplain to the Archbishop of Canterbury from 1501, and quickly rose through the ecclesiastical ranks to become Archbishop of York in 1514. A year later he became both Cardinal and Lord Chancellor of England.

In 1518 Pope Leo X honoured Wolsey with the status of *legate a latere*, outranking the legatine status held by every Archbishop of Canterbury. In

1524 this title was, uniquely, given for life. This honour was eventually to be used against him when in 1529 he was charged with *praemunire* (invoking papal authority over that of the King) and ousted from office.

Cardinal Wolsey worked hard politically on behalf of Henry and equally hard in his management of the church. However, he was resented politically, and his amassed powers and riches gave rise to suspicion and envy. The ostentation of his household at Hampton Court and York Place did nothing to dispel the resentment.

Wolsey twice restructured the King's Privy Chamber in order to protect himself from hostile courtiers, but he met his downfall over the issue of the annulment of Henry's first marriage. Wolsey was planning a diplomatic second marriage to a French bride for the King, but was unable to control Anne Boleyn, whose anti-clerical and anti-Wolsey propaganda eventually led the King to dismiss Wolsey from all his offices in October 1529.

When Wolsey was deposed on a charge of a *praemunire,* he was forced to restrict his interests to purely church affairs. However, a year later he interfered in diplomacy and was denounced as a traitor. He died at Leicester in November 1530, on his way to London to answer the charge of treachery.

HENRY VIII WITH CARDINAL WOLSEY

FACT, FICTION AND FABLE

The Masque

Before the 16th century, performances at court were similar to those in the theatre. Then, influenced by developments in Italy, court entertainment developed along different lines. While professional actors on the Elizabethan stage were concentrating on acting and drama, court entertainment was based on spectacle and scenery, which in turn developed into masque, a courtly entertainment involving dance, speech, song and instrumental music.

Masque existed to please and flatter royal spectators and to suit the court taste for chivalric allegory. Masques were often staged to impress foreign visitors; as well as extolling the virtues of the host, they were outstanding in splendour and brilliance, often at the expense of dialogue. Ben Jonson (the first poet laureate) wrote several celebrated masques but gave up, not wishing, as he said, to compete with the carpenter and the scene-painter.

The Italian Andrea Pozzo described masque as 'making the spectators themselves see a thing which they denied could be done'. Pozzo was an expert on perspective, which had been used in Italian masque since 1551, when Sebastian Serlio had shown how it could make the stage seem much larger than it really was.

Serlio's ideas, and those of other Italians, were brought back to England by the architect and stage designer Inigo Jones, who took the use of scenery and stage machinery to unprecedented levels.

Jones staged many expensive and spectacular masques for Charles I at the Banqueting House. In 1640 he collaborated with Sir William Davenant and produced *Salmacida Spolia*, in which both Charles and his Queen played superbly dressed and ingeniously mechanised parts. The accounts show expenses of over £500 for the King's costume, the equivalent of about £75,000 today.

THE EXECUTION OF CHARLES I

The most famous event to have taken place in the Banqueting House at Whitehall is the execution of Charles I on 30 January 1649.

Charles had been tried for treason in Westminster Hall and convicted by Cromwell's Puritans, after which he was held under house arrest at St James's Palace while the scaffold was erected outside the Banqueting House. His wife, Henrietta Maria, had fled to France, and the day before the execution his two youngest children, Princess Elizabeth, who was thirteen, and Henry, Duke of Gloucester, who was nine, were brought to say goodbye to their father.

On the day of the execution, a small procession set off across St James's Park to Whitehall, surrounded by an escort of halberdiers. Spectators gathered on rooftops to watch. It was a bitterly cold day and Charles wore two shirts, not wanting to shiver in case the crowd mistook his shivering for fear.

The King was persuaded to drink a glass of claret and eat a little bread. He walked through the very room in which he had commissioned Rubens to paint the magnificent ceiling panels, and stepped out on to the scaffold from a window. He made a brief speech, declaring himself to be 'the martyr of the people', and asked the executioner to wait until he gave the signal that he was ready. The barrier around the scaffold had been draped in black cloth so the spectators saw nothing but the swift descent of the axe. When it fell, a terrible moan arose from the crowd.

EXECUTION OF
CHARLES I

FACT, FICTION AND FABLE

Changes to the Calendar

Some history books record the execution of Charles I as taking place in January 1648, others as 1649. The reason for this discrepancy is that, until 1752, the official new year in Britain began on 25 March, which had been the date of the equinox at the time the Julian calendar was drawn up. However, New Year's Day was popularly (though unofficially) acknowledged as 1 January, and it was customary to write both years for dates between 1 January and 25 March. Thus, 5 January 1752 in popular reckoning would have been written 5 January 1751/52: officially 1751 but popularly 1752.

Then, in a 1752 Act of Parliament, Britain finally accepted the Gregorian calendar with the New Year starting on 1 January. This involved removing eleven days from the old calendar in order to bring it into line with the rest of Europe. The complication was that historians recording an event that happened between 1 January and 25 March in a year prior to 1753, would place the date in the official old year (30 January 1648 in Charles's case); after 1753, the same date would be officially in the new year (January was then in 1649).

In the year after the *Act for Regulating the Commencement of the Year, and for Correcting the Calendar now in Use*, London bankers insisted on paying their taxes not only at what would have been year end under the old system (25 March), but eleven days later to account for the eleven days which had been removed from the calendar. Since then 5 April has remained the end of the tax year in Britain.

In 1582 Pope Gregory had decreed that his calendar should replace the flawed Julian calendar which had been in use since the time of Julius Caesar and which had accrued an error of ten days. Britain did not comply with the papal bull until 170 years later, by which time the old calendar had strayed by a further day. Modern travellers to the continent have to put their watches forward an hour, but for those 170 years Britain was ten (or eleven) *days* behind! When the eleven days were eventually removed from the calendar (Thursday 14 September 1752 followed Wednesday 2 September), there were riots in some parts of the country and amusement or apathy in others.

ST JAMES'S PALACE

A Brief History

1532
The Tudor palace of St James's was built by John Molton for Henry VIII on the site of a hospital for female lepers, called 'St James's in the Fields'. The hospital became a convent but was dissolved in 1532 when Henry had acquired it, after which he drained the surrounding marshes and enclosed the fields, thus creating St James's Park, the oldest of the royal parks.

There are various theories as to why Henry built a palace here when he was already established at Whitehall Palace nearby: one is that it was a hunting lodge and private retreat for him and his lover, Anne Boleyn; another is that it was for Edward, the Prince of Wales.

1623–27
There have been many alterations, rebuildings and additions to the palace, including the addition of a Catholic chapel designed by Inigo Jones for Charles I. Built for Henrietta Maria, Charles' consort, the Queen's Chapel was based on Palladio's restoration of the Temple of Venus in Rome and was a new departure for English architecture.

1642–49
During the Civil War, the palace was used as a barracks, and Cromwell began selling the art treasures which Charles I had collected here. The palace was also the scene of the escape of Charles I's younger son, Prince James, after his capture at the Battle of Edgehill, and Charles I spent the night before his execution here.

1660–85
After the Restoration, Charles II refurbished St James's Palace and it was used for state occasions. He also restored the park after the depredations of the Civil War and a great storm on the night of Cromwell's death in 1658, extending it by 36 acres. St James's Park became the first royal park; in it Charles created many features in his father's memory, including Birdcage Walk, to help expunge the tragic memory of Charles I's walk across the park to his execution. The canal became one of his favourite places, where he could often be seen accompanied by his mistresses, walking his dogs and sometimes even swimming.

1698–
Whitehall Palace was burned down four years before the death of William III, and it was during the reign of his successor, Queen Anne, that St James's became the home of the court and the official residence of the sovereign. St James's was extended for Queen Anne by Christopher Wren.

1749–66
Despite Wren's improvements, St James's Palace did not impress foreign visitors: the King of Prussia reported in 1749 that 'the King's lodging house is crazy, smoky and dirty', and by 1766 the palace had become an object of reproach in the kingdom. It was nevertheless retained as the official seat of the monarchy for lack of a suitable alternative.

1840
Queen Victoria married Prince Albert in the Chapel Royal at St James's on 10 February 1840.

St James's Palace was originally built for Henry VIII but did not become the principal royal residence until the very end of the reign of William III, after the fire in 1698 which destroyed Whitehall Palace.

QUEEN VICTORIA AT ST JAMES'S
Queen Victoria used Buckingham Palace as her official residence, but St James's was still used for all state functions and ceremonial, and in 1840 it was the setting for a royal wedding. Victoria had proposed to her beloved Albert, and she decided that the wedding should take place at St James's Palace, in the Chapel Royal where she had been confirmed.

Victoria and Albert both spent the night before the wedding at St James's, to the distaste of the Duchess of Kent, who thought it 'indelicate' that they should sleep under the same roof before they were married.

The ceremony took place on 10 February 1840; Queen Victoria wore white satin with Honiton lace, a diamond necklace and earrings, and a sapphire brooch which was a gift from Prince Albert. The twelve bridesmaids carried white roses.

Three attempts to assassinate Victoria were made close to St James's, all on Constitution Hill in Green Park. On 10 June 1840 a man called Oxford shot at her; two years later, on 30 May 1842, a man called Francis did the same, and, seven years after that, on 19 May 1849, the papers reported that 'an idiot named Hamilton' had tried to kill her.

FACT, FICTION AND FABLE

The Escape of Prince James
In 1642, during the Civil War, Prince James (the third, but second surviving son of Charles I), was captured at the Battle of Edgehill and brought to St James's Palace where he was guarded by Cromwell's men.

He escaped from them by playing a regular game of hide and seek with his captors in the garden. Day by day he gradually extended his absence by finding progressively more difficult hiding places.

Finally, he chained up his dog who might otherwise have followed him, obtained the key to the garden gate from a gardener and slipped into St James's Park where friends were waiting in a coach with a disguise for him.

By the time the guards discovered he had escaped, he had gone downriver to Gravesend from where he set sail for the continent. He returned at the Restoration and was later crowned King James II.

ST JAMES'S PALACE
This tudor palace was built for Henry VIII over 450 years ago, but he would still recognise the gatehouse if he saw it today.

BUCKINGHAM PALACE

A Brief History

1702–5
The first building on the site was Buckingham House, built between 1702 and 1705 by William Winde for John Sheffield, 1st Duke of Buckingham and Normanby.

1762
Buckingham's son sold the house to George III in 1762 for £28,000. George was newly married and wanted a retreat from what he called 'that dust trap', St James's Palace.

1775
The King intended Buckingham House to be both a family house and a dower house for his queen, Charlotte Sophia. When it was legally settled on the Queen in 1775, in exchange for Somerset House which went to the nation, its name was changed to Queen's House. Gradually, the modest house was enlarged to accommodate the King's collection of books and his growing family.

1820–1830
The Prince Regent had been living at Carlton House but soon after coming to the throne in 1820, as George IV, he announced that it was not grand enough for the King of England. He decided that a new palace must be built on the site of Queen's House, but the Commons would only allow him funds for the repair and improvement of the existing house. The King approached his friend John Nash to convert it for him. The cost of Nash's conversion soon spiralled. Wellington was Prime Minister, and although he disapproved, he could not force the abandonment of the work; the cost eventually rose to more than three times the original estimate. The new house was renamed Buckingham Palace.

1830
The press reported that Buckingham Palace would be ready for the King's occupation by August 1830 but in June he died. The Treasury almost immediately withdrew Nash's commission and Edward Blore was called upon to make the palace habitable.

1834
William IV disliked Buckingham Palace and never lived there. When the Palace of Westminster burned down in 1834, he offered Buckingham Palace as a new Parliament House, a permanent gift from the Crown. Parliament, however, declined the offer.

1837
When Queen Victoria succeeded to the throne in 1837, Buckingham Palace was still barely habitable; nothing worked. But under Victoria the work begun by George IV was finally completed and Buckingham Palace has been the official London residence of the sovereign ever since.

1913
The original stucco façade of the palace had collapsed, due to pollution, and the present Portland stone façade was commissioned by George V to replace it. The railings, Queen's Gardens and Victoria Memorial were also erected about this time.

1940
King George VI and Queen Elizabeth had courageously stayed in London throughout the Second World War. On 13 September 1940 Buckingham Palace was bombed and the chapel 'wrecked'. Queen Elizabeth (now HM The Queen Mother) remarked at the time, 'I'm glad we have been bombed; I feel I can look the East End in the face.'

1993
In 1993, Buckingham Palace was opened to the public for the first time; some 400,000 visitors a year are now able to view the state rooms designed by Blore and Nash. When the Queen is in residence the Royal Standard flies at the palace masthead.

Although Buckingham Palace is one of the most famous buildings in the world, and the official residence of the monarch in London, its royal role is remarkably recent. A mulberry garden once occupied the site, planted as part of James I's policy of encouraging the silk industry in England. Unfortunately, he planted black mulberries; it is white mulberries that the silkworms feed on.

GEORGE III

George III began the royal connection with what is now Buckingham Palace, buying it as a family home but intending it also as a dower house for Queen Charlotte. George and Charlotte had six daughters and ten sons, including the future George IV and William IV.

George was the son of Frederick, Prince of Wales and Augusta. He succeeded his grandfather in 1760 at the age of 22, and was crowned a year later. He prided himself on his patriotism, and during his reign Nelson defeated the combined French and Spanish fleets at Trafalgar. However, it was also under George that the American colonists, to his distress, successfully defended their Declaration of Independence, in 1776.

'Farmer George' delighted in his nickname, which reflected the time he spent on his experimental farms in Windsor Park. But George III was also a passionate collector, especially of books. He kept adding rooms to Queen's House, some to accommodate his growing family, and also libraries to accommodate his books.

George III is, however, perhaps best known for his madness, which manifested itself in what are now believed to be the symptoms of porphyria, the 'royal malady', although suspicion has also fallen on lead poisoning from the drinking vessels George used. His first attack came in 1764, only three years into his reign; the last attack, in 1810, proved to be permanent and his son George was proclaimed Prince Regent in 1811. George III died at Windsor on 29 January 1820.

BUCKINGHAM PALACE
The new Portland stone façade was designed by Sir Aston Webb
and erected in 1913 for George V.

GEORGE IV

George IV, the former Prince Regent, was responsible for commissioning the rebuilding of Queen's House as Buckingham Palace. Unfortunately, he died before the palace was completed, so he never actually lived there.

As a young prince, George's good looks, high spirits and agreeable manners made him popular. He became a darling of fashionable society, among whom he was known as 'Prinny'. By the time he was twenty-one, an act of Parliament was required to pay off his debts and shortly afterwards he secretly married one of his mistresses, the Catholic Mrs Fitzherbert. The marriage was illegal; if he married a Roman Catholic he would be excluded from the succession, and under the Royal Marriage Act of 1772, descendants of George II were forbidden to marry under the age of twenty-five without the permission of the monarch. George subsequently married Caroline of Brunswick in 1795, but only because Parliament again promised to pay his debts. It is said that when George first set eyes on Caroline, he turned pale and asked for brandy, and that he only got through the marriage ceremony by getting drunk. Their dislike for each other was intense and led to separation within a year and to Caroline being barred from the coronation. George also tried to deprive Caroline of the title of queen but the Bill was dropped by the House of Lords after its third reading. The couple did, nevertheless, produce an heir to the throne in Princess Charlotte, who tragically died in childbirth at the age of eighteen.

George was proclaimed Prince Regent in 1811 and succeeded to the throne nine year later in January 1820. As King, George continued his notorious extravagance; he was castigated for his excesses but posterity is grateful for some of his projects, most notably the Brighton Pavilion. He was essentially an amiable, self-indulgent dandy with romantic illusions about himself: in later life he even claimed to have fought at the Battle of Waterloo. When he realised that his listeners doubted his story, he asked the Duke of Wellington for confirmation. The Duke tactfully replied, 'I have often heard Your Majesty say so.'

FACT, FICTION AND FABLE

John Nash

When George IV succeeded to the throne in 1820, John Nash was already a friend and his favourite architect. Sir John Soane was the architect officially responsible for the royal palaces but the King instructed that all plans relating to Buckingham Palace (then Queen's House) be transferred to Nash.

Nash, born in 1752, was a brilliant but slapdash architect, responsible for laying out Regent's Park and its terraces, Regent Street, Carlton House Terrace, Trafalgar Square and St James's Park. He rushed into his new commisson without building a model, and was disappointed when he saw his design materialise, later admitting that the wings flanking the main part of the building were a failure. Criticism was also directed at the dome on the garden front, which was visible above the portico on the main front and was described as 'a common slop pail turned upside down'.

Nash was supported throughout by George IV. As the King urged Nash on, the building gained in splendour but the budget ran out of control. By the end, the cost had risen from an initial estimate of £200,000 to nearly £700,000, excluding the cost of the Marble Arch, which originally stood in front of the palace.

George IV died in June 1830, before the completion of Buckingham Palace. Four months later the Treasury withdrew Nash's commission and called upon Edward Blore to finish the palace and make it habitable. John Nash died in 1835.

Edward Blore

Edward Blore was 'discovered' by Walter Scott, who employed him to remodel his house, Abbotsford, in the Gothic style. Born in 1787, Blore was closely associated with the Gothic Revival. He was a well-respected architect of country houses and was called upon by Parliament to replace John Nash and to complete Nash's work on Buckingham Palace.

Blore removed the eastern pavilions built by Nash and replaced the much-criticised dome with an attic. However, the public was still not impressed and one critic of 1832 (an anonymous architect) wrote: 'Is it possible that the nation... should provide for the metropolitan residence of his Britannic Majesty such a gimcrack as Buckingham House?'

Blore converted the south-west pavilion into a chapel for Queen Victoria and designed a whimsical Swiss cottage in the garden. He also modified and completed work on Nash's Marble Arch, which commemorates the victories at Trafalgar and Waterloo.

The state apartments of the palace are the work of Nash, Blore or a combination of both; the grand staircase is by Nash while the state dining room is Blore's. The ballroom range was added in 1853 by James Pannethorne who had trained under his uncle, John Nash.

From 1827 until his retirement, Blore was Surveyor to Westminster Abbey. He died in 1879.

QUEEN VICTORIA

Queen Victoria was the first monarch to make Buckingham Palace her official residence, moving there from Kensington Palace within three weeks of her accession to the throne on 20 June 1837.

The Princess Victoria was born at Kensington Palace on 24 May 1819. Her father was Edward, Duke of Kent, and her mother Princess Victoria of Saxe-Coburg, sister of Leopold, King of Belgium. Her reign of 63 years was the longest of any British monarch; by the time of her death in 1901, few of her subjects were old enough to remember life under any other monarch. At the time of Victoria's accession to the throne in 1837 (at the age of eighteen), the horse was the fastest form of transport; by the time of her death, trains were being challenged by the car.

The role of the monarchy as it is today was established during Victoria's reign: much of her greatness lies in the fact that she restored its dignity and reputation and gave it a new place in a changing world. Although the Crown lost almost all executive power, the monarchy gained greatly in prestige; Victoria was perceived as representing all the people in her empire, not just an aristocratic clique. Victoria's image was often contradictory, not least in her role as queen, where she was at once a grand symbol of the national heritage and a loving wife and mother with whom her subjects could identify. This dual role is one which her successors have played with varying success.

Victoria's popularity waned when she went into seclusion after the death of Albert, but, lured back into public life by Benjamin Disraeli, her standing rose with the years; her Golden and Diamond Jubilees (1887 and 1897) showed monarchy at its most theatrical, both occasions providing dazzling imperial pageants with Victoria at their centre.

Victoria had four sons, including the future Edward VII, and five daughters. She died at Osborne House on the Isle of Wight on 22 January 1901.

It is hard to imagine the English language without the adjective 'Victorian', or the famous phrase which in later life the Queen denied uttering: 'We are not amused.' Legend has it that the royal 'We', coined by Victoria, resulted from her reluctance to dissociate herself from Prince Albert, even after his death.

THE VICTORIA MEMORIAL

After Victoria's death, a committee was set up by Viscount Esher (who had superintended her funeral) to decide on a memorial. A memorial fund was established and architects were invited to submit proposals. Sir Aston Webb, whose design for Admiralty Arch had already been accepted, was chosen and planned the siting of a statue by Thomas Brock in front of the palace.

A CLOSER LOOK

MARBLE ARCH

Marble Arch once formed the gateway to Buckingham Palace. John Nash's original design for George IV gave the palace a three-sided open courtyard with a huge gateway based on the famous Arch of Constantine in Rome.

Nash and the King decided that a marble arch would be preferable to the Bath stone from which the palace was built, so Nash sent an agent to Italy to purchase Ravaccione marble straight from the quarry at Seravezzo. The gateway was intended as the culmination of a triumphal route to the palace but it was found that royal coaches could not conveniently pass through.

After Nash's dismissal in 1830, Edward Blore enclosed the courtyard by adding the east wing, which involved moving Marble Arch to its present position at the top of Park Lane, where it was re-erected in 1851.

BUCKINGHAM PALACE
The Throne Room.

KENSINGTON

The most obvious association between the Crown and this part of London is Kensington Palace.

However, there are links also with Hyde Park and the much less well known Albertropolis. The park is the oldest

element and was formerly a royal hunting forest, while the palace has been a royal residence since the reign of

William and Mary. Yet is is the creation of Albertropolis which is the unique feature in the story of Kensington.

Named after Prince Albert, Queen Victoria's consort, this whole area was built on the foundations of one

remarkable event, The Great Exhibition of 1851. This ambitious scheme was ridiculed at its outset, yet turned

out to be a phenomenal success. The profits from the Great Exhibition were subsequently used to buy the land on

which the Museums and eventually the Royal Albert Hall were built. An extraordinary legacy of an

extraordinary man.

THE VICTORIA & ALBERT MUSEUM
Originally called the South Kensington Museum, the V&A was renamed in 1899
when Queen Victoria laid the foundation stone of a new extension to the museum.

ROYAL BOROUGH OF KENSINGTON

A Brief History

1086
The name Kensington is of Anglo-Saxon origin and is recorded in the Domesday Book as Chenesit. It is thought that the village grew up on rising ground around what is now St Mary Abbots Church. At the time of the Norman conquest, the manor came into the ownership of the De Vere family, who were later Earls of Oxford. It remained in the family until the early 16th century.

16th century
Kensington was a rural parish, with arable land to the north and market gardens and nurseries established in the late 16th century to the south.

17th century
From the early 17th century, the wealthy began to build mansions on the high ground between Kensington and Notting Hill; these had all the advantages of a country estate but were within easy reach of London. Holland House was built in 1606, Campden House in 1612, and in 1689 William III bought Nottingham House and commissioned Wren and Hawksmoor to convert it into Kensington Palace.

1705
In his book *Antiquities of Middlesex*, John Bowack

describes Kensington as being 'resorted to by persons of quality . . . inhabited by gentry and persons of note; there is also an abundance of shopkeepers and . . . artificers . . . which makes it appear rather like a part of London, than a country village'.

1851
There was public outcry when Hyde Park was the site of the Great Exhibition in 1851.

19th century
During the 19th century, the urban spread of London made land more profitable for building, and Kensington changed from being a rural parish with 8,556 inhabitants (1801 census) to a metropolitan borough of 176,628 (1901 census). Acres of new housing were developed.

1900
In 1900 Kensington was given the status of a metropolitan borough, and Queen Victoria was requested to confer the title 'royal' on the new borough in recognition of her birthplace. She died before it could be officially implemented, but her heir, Edward VII, conferred the title on her behalf in 1901.

1965
The present borough was formed by a merger with Chelsea in 1965.

Kensington was given the prefix 'royal' in honour of the birth there of Queen Victoria, and is one of only two royal boroughs in London, the other being Kingston. Kensington is home to three of Britain's best-known museums: the V&A, the Science Museum and the Natural History Museum. The museum area became known as 'Albertropolis' after Prince Albert established several artistic and scientific institutions here, using money generated from the Great Exhibition of 1851.

QUEEN VICTORIA AND KENSINGTON

The Great Exhibition was the brainchild of Henry Cole, who was assistant keeper of the Public Record Office. The purpose of the exhibition was 'to encourage art and industry to work together with the best technology and creativity in order to improve lifestyles'; it was effectively the biggest trade show the world had ever seen. In 1850 a Royal Commission, presided over by Prince Albert, was appointed to raise the money needed.

When Queen Victoria gave permission for Hyde Park to be used as the site for the exhibition, there was public outcry; people felt that the area would become a 'bivouac of all vagabonds' and were afraid that Kensington would become uninhabitable.

A competition was held for the design of the exhibition. Some 234 entries were received, and the winner was Joseph Paxton's design for a crystal palace based on the conservatory at Chatsworth House, where he was head gardener. Over 2,000 men were employed to construct the monumental building, which covered 19 acres and used 4,000 tons of iron and 400 tons of glass. Trees in the park were incorporated into the design, but the numerous sparrows which

accompanied them proved to be a problem: their droppings spattered the exhibits until the Duke of Wellington suggested introducing sparrowhawks.

Once built, it was necessary to test whether the Crystal Palace could withstand the thousands of expected visitors: squads of soldiers were marched in and ordered to jump up and down shouting at the tops of their voices. The building withstood the tests and was opened by Queen Victoria on 1 May 1851. She was so impressed that she visited the exhibition 34 times during the first three months. Categories of exhibits were: Raw Materials, Machinery and Invention, Sculpture and Plastic Arts, and Manufacture, and exhibits came from all over the world; they included jewels (one of which was the famous Koh-i-noor diamond), leather goods, textiles, china, glass, cutlery, household gadgets and engines of all descriptions.

Between 1 May and 11 October 1851, when the exhibition closed, it was visited by over six million people, who came from all over the country, including one eighty-four-year-old woman who had walked all the way from Cornwall.

The following year, the Crystal Palace was taken down and re-erected near Sydenham in south London. It was unfortunately destroyed by fire on 30 November 1936, but the area still carries its name.

THE ROYAL ALBERT HALL

*The hall was to have been called the Central Hall of Arts and Sciences, but when the foundation stone
was laid by Queen Victoria in 1867, she prefaced the title with the words 'Royal Albert'.*

The exhibition was a success, and Prince Albert was given the title Consort for his involvement with it. A large profit was made, which Albert used to fulfil one of his dreams: an establishment which would extend the influence of science and art to industry. His aim was to provide museums, concert halls, colleges, schools and premises for learned societies. The Commissioners of the Great Exhibition chose a 200-acre site in South Kensington which at the time still consisted mainly of market gardens. People joked that the commission was 'sinking money into a cabbage garden'. Albert persuaded several existing institutions to relocate, including the Museum of Manufactures and the School of Design (a forerunner of the Royal College of Arts), thus forming the South Kensington Museum, which opened in 1857.

In 1899, 38 years after Albert's death, Queen Victoria laid the foundation stone of a new extension to the museum. It was to be the last important official duty of her reign and it was appropriate that she gave the institution a new name: the Victoria & Albert Museum. It was her final opportunity to pay homage to life with her beloved husband.

After Albert's death in 1861, a public fund was set up to finance a memorial and to realise Albert's scheme for a hall with libraries, exhibition rooms and an enormous lecture theatre. Not enough money could be found for both the hall and a memorial, so Henry Cole proposed financing the hall by selling a 999-year leasehold of seats. Over 1,300 seats were sold, at £100 each, which entitled the owners to free attendance at every performance – a scheme which is still in force today. Queen Victoria bought 20 seats, which make up the present Royal Box. The Commissioners of the 1851 Exhibition, who are still the hall's landlords, donated the site at a peppercorn rent of 1s (10p) a year.

The foundation stone of the hall was laid by Queen Victoria in 1867. It was to have been called the Central Hall of Arts and Sciences, but in her speech the Queen prefaced the title with Royal Albert. She next visited four years later for the grand opening ceremony, at which she was so overcome with emotion that she could not finish her speech and the Prince of Wales stepped forward to declare the hall officially open.

THE SCULPTURE GALLERY AT THE V&A
The 'Three Graces' are to the left of the picture, with 'Theseus and the Minotaur' in the foreground. Both are by Antonio Canova (1757–1822).

THE CAST COURT AT THE V&A

In the background is a copy of Michelangelo's 'David'. When Queen Victoria visited the museum a specially designed fig leaf was strategically placed to save the Queen from embarrassment.

HYDE PARK

Hyde Park takes its name from the Saxon word meaning 100 acres, but is now more than three times that size. The land was bequeathed to the monks at Westminster, soon after the Conquest, as a source of meat, but at the Dissolution of the Monasteries, Henry VIII took possession of the land and retained it for hunting. James I opened the park to the public, and in the 17th century it became a fashionable place of entertainment, especially for the annual May Day festivities.

To the north-east of the park stood the Tyburn Tree, which from the 12th century was one of the most famous execution sites in London. In 1571 the tree was replaced with a triangular wooden scaffold which could be used to hang up to eight people at a time.

In 1642 forts were built in the park to defend the city against Royalist attacks. In 1652 the park was sold on the order of the Parliamentarians, and coach races became popular. At the Restoration in 1660, Charles II took it back and enclosed it, but the park nevertheless continued to be plagued by highwaymen. It was also a favourite place for duels.

Queen Caroline, wife of George II, was responsible for uniting Hyde Park and Kensington Gardens, and in 1730 she had the Westbourne dammed to form the Serpentine. In 1814 a great fair was held to celebrate the end of the war with France, and in 1821 firework displays and balloon ascents marked the coronation of George IV. During the 19th century, gates, a bridge over the Serpentine, and the Ranger's Lodge were built. In 1872 the legal right to assembly resulted in freedom of speech at Speakers' Corner. Statues, memorials, fountains, the Marble Arch and a restaurant and art gallery have since been introduced.

In an area known as the Dell, at the east end of the Serpentine, is the so-called Standing Stone, which local legend says was brought to Hyde Park from Stonehenge by Charles I. In fact it is a 7-ton piece of Cornish stone, part of a drinking fountain which once stood in the Dell.

A CLOSER LOOK

THE ALBERT MEMORIAL

Erected after his death to commemorate Prince Albert, the Albert Memorial was designed by George Gilbert Scott, and throughout its history has been loved and hated with almost equal passion. Queen Victoria chose Scott's plans from among those submitted by the eminent architects of the day and in 1863 Parliament voted £50,000 towards the building of the monument.

On 1 July 1872 Victoria was able to inspect the memorial, which was complete except for the central statue of the Prince. The Queen never expressed an opinion of the monument, but Scott was knighted. The public were admitted on 3 July, although, due to the death of the first sculptor, Baron Marochetti, it was not until four years later, in 1876, that the 14 ft bronze statue of the Prince was finally erected. It was completed by John Foley.

The memorial stands 175 ft high and includes seven tiers of statues, sculpture and bas-reliefs representing the continents of the world and all manner of human achievements, achievers and ideals. On the corners of the podium are Agriculture, Commerce, Manufactures and Engineering; around the base are 169 life-size figures, with painters on the east side, architects on the north, musicians and poets on the south and sculptors on the west; on the pillars are Astronomy, Chemistry, Geology and Geometry, with Rhetoric,

Medicine, Philosophy and Physiology above them; in the arches are Poetry, Painting, Architecture and Sculpture; and in niches on the spires are Faith, Hope, Charity and Humility, with Fortitude, Prudence, Justice and Temperance at the corners. At the centre of the memorial is the statue of Prince Albert, who is shown seated and reading a catalogue of the 1851 Exhibition.

In 1990 the statues were removed so that the rusting iron frame could be repaired. The cost of the restoration was met by the Department of the Environment, English Heritage and the Victorian Society. The renovated memorial was unveiled by Queen Elizabeth II on 31 October 1998.

KENSINGTON PALACE

Kensington Palace was originally a Jacobean house built for Sir George Coppin. It was later bought by William III's Secretary of State, the Earl of Nottingham, at which time it became known as Nottingham House. Queen Mary bought the house in 1689 for £18,000, and it subsequently became a favoured royal residence and the birthplace of Queen Victoria.

A Brief History

1689
William and Mary both disliked the palace at Whitehall, where William suffered badly from asthma. They kept Whitehall for ceremonial occasions, and moved out to Hampton Court where they began to redesign much of the palace and gardens. In 1689 they bought Nottingham House, the grounds of which appealed to the King's passion for garden design. The house was intended as a private retreat and winter residence.

Sir Christopher Wren was commissioned to reconstruct the house, and Nicholas Hawksmoor was appointed Clerk of Works. Queen Mary, impatient to move in, often went to Kensington to 'hasten the workmen'. By Christmas that year, the house was still far from finished but the royal family were able to move in to what became known as Kensington Palace.

1690
In February 1690, Evelyn described the palace as being 'a patch'd building', but by August Mary was able to tell William, 'Kensington is ready'. Improvements continued and the palace rose slightly in Evelyn's estimation: he described the gardens as 'very delicious' and the house as 'very noble, tho not greate'.

William had a private road built across Hyde Park to the palace. It was lit by 300 lanterns hung from the trees, and was the first road in England to be lit at night. Originally called the 'Route du Roi', the name became corrupted to what is now Rotten Row.

The royal gardeners, Henry Wise and George London, laid out the gardens to the south of the palace to Mary's instructions, with clipped box and yew in formal Dutch patterns.

1702–14
William III's successor, Queen Anne, also lived at Kensington Palace, which was by then seen as the official residence of the monarch. Queen Anne lived there with her close friend Sarah Churchill, the Duchess of Marlborough, and died at Kensington Palace on 1 August 1714 of a stroke brought on by over-eating. The Queen had grown so stout by her death that her huge coffin was almost cubic in shape.

1714–27
George I liked Kensington Palace because it reminded him of his palace at Herrenhausen in Hanover. He brought a large household with him, including his mistresses, and built three new State Rooms from 1718–21. William Kent painted the Grand Staircase, which depicted various members of George's court, including the bizarre character Peter the Wild Boy.

Kent was responsible for much of the painting at Kensington Palace, securing the commission by undercutting the official royal artist, James Thornhill.

1727–60
George II and Queen Caroline used Kensington as their principal residence.

1760–
George III preferred St James's Palace and, later, Buckingham House (which became Buckingham Palace), and after 1760 Kensington Palace began to fall into disrepair.

1798
George III's son, the Duke of Kent, was allocated rooms at Kensington in 1798, and expensive alterations were made by James Wyatt. However, shortly afterwards the Duke moved abroad.

24 May 1819
The Duke of Kent returned to Kensington with his wife, Princess Victoria of Saxe-Coburg-Saalfeld, so that their daughter could be born in England. On 24 May the future Queen Victoria was born at the palace, and was christened there in June.

20 June 1837
Princess Victoria was called from her bed at 6 am by the Archbishop of Canterbury and the Lord Chamberlain to be told that she was queen. The following day she held her accession council at Kensington Palace and within three weeks had moved to Buckingham Palace.

1867–80
The Duke and Duchess of Teck lived at Kensington Palace from 1867 to 1880, and their daughter, later Queen Mary, was born there in 1867.

1880–1939
Queen Victoria's sixth child, Princess Louise, lived at the palace.

1950–75
The London Museum was housed in the State Apartments.

Present day
Several members of the royal family have apartments at Kensington Palace, including the Prince of Wales, Princess Margaret, the Duke and Duchess of Gloucester, Prince and Princess Michael of Kent, and Princess Alice.

KENSINGTON PALACE

The Palace is divided into a number of apartments, each allocated to members of the royal family.
This use of the palace led the Duke of Windsor, formerly Edward VIII, to christen it 'the aunt heap'.

WILLIAM III

This bronze statue of William III by Heinrich Baucke, erected at Kensington Palace in 1907, was presented by Kaiser Wilhelm II to his uncle, Edward VII, for 'the British nation'. King William died at Kensington Palace after retiring there to convalesce from a riding accident at Hampton Court.

QUEEN VICTORIA

In the grounds of Kensington Palace stands this statue of Queen Victoria at the time of her accession, sculpted by her fourth daughter, Princess Louise. The statue was commissioned by the residents of Kensington to commemorate Victoria's Golden Jubilee in 1887, and was erected in 1893.

QUEEN ANNE AND THE DUCHESS OF MARLBOROUGH

Queen Anne lived at Kensington Palace in the company of her friend Sarah Churchill, the Duchess of Marlborough. The two women had been friends since childhood, and Anne had always admired Sarah's vitality and toughness. When Sarah was made Mistress of the Robes and Keeper of the Privy Purse, she was also awarded large apartments at Kensington Palace. Anne and Sarah often used assumed names, which allowed them to correspond with an informality not usually seen between queen and courtier. The Queen was referred to as Mrs Morley, and Sarah was known as Mrs Freeman.

Their intimate friendship nevertheless came to a bitter end. The Duchess was a strong supporter of the Whig party; the Tory party, searching for someone to balance her powerful influence over the Queen, managed to manoeuvre another lady in waiting into the Queen's affections: Lady Masham. When Anne's husband, George, died in 1708, Sarah was unsympathetic but Lady Masham was there to comfort her and it soon became obvious that favour had changed.

The Duchess wrote reproachful letters which so angered the Queen that in 1711 she invited Sarah to the palace, where they quarrelled, and Sarah was dismissed as Keeper of the Privy Purse. The Duchess complained that she had been 'kept waiting like a Scotch lady with a petition' and told Anne that she would suffer for her inhumanity. As a final insult, Sarah also claimed £16,000 back pay which she said she had earned by enduring so many hours of boredom.

They never spoke again and Queen Anne died at Kensington Palace three years later.

The most significant political event of Queen Anne's reign was the 1707 Act of Union between England and Scotland, which made Anne the first sovereign of the United Kingdom.

FACT, FICTION AND FABLE

Lady Sarah Lennox

Lady Sarah Lennox first saw George II when she was a small child, walking with her governess in Kensington Gardens. She ran to the King and addressed him in French; he was charmed, and Sarah soon went regularly to Kensington Palace to amuse him.

Sarah was brought up nearby at Holland House, named after Lord Holland who had won royal favour with Charles I but changed his allegiances many times between King and Parliament; this fickleness resulted in the confiscation of Holland House, and his execution by Parliament in 1649, during the Civil War. The house was eventually returned to Holland's widow who had plays privately performed there to combat her loneliness, in defiance of the laws established under the Commonwealth. London theatres had been closed by the Puritans, and Holland House was one of the private houses which illegally helped to keep the spirit of theatre alive. Plays are performed there to this day: the ruins of the house are used as an outdoor theatre during the summer.

After spending some time in Ireland, Sarah Lennox returned to Holland House at the age of fourteen, and was immediately invited to Kensington Palace. The King seemed disappointed with how she had grown up; he thought her shy and that her silence reflected stupidity.

But the effect on his grandson, the Prince of Wales and future George III, was the opposite: he found Sarah charming and began to court her. Sarah's guardian tried to encourage the situation by having her rake hay in the grounds of Holland House so that the Prince would see her on his daily ride past the house. The ploy worked and the prince was smitten, but Sarah was destined not to be queen. She broke her leg, which took her out of the court circle for several weeks, during which time the Prince's mother, Augusta, arranged his marriage to Princess Charlotte of Mecklenburg.

KENSINGTON GARDENS

KENSINGTON GARDENS

Kensington Gardens, originally the gardens of the palace, were laid out by George London in the formal Dutch style for William and Mary, half of it as a parterre with clipped evergreens, and half as a 'wilderness' with walks. The planting was subsequently uprooted, and the gardens greatly extended and laid out in a more English style under Queen Anne. In the reign of George II, Queen Caroline, working with William Kent, made further improvements, establishing the Round Pond in 1728, and joining together the marshy ponds of the Westbourne river to make the Serpentine in 1730.

George II opened the gardens on Saturdays to 'respectably dressed people', and the Broad Walk became as fashionable as the Mall had been a century before.

Early one morning, while he was on a solitary walk in Kensington Gardens, George II was robbed. A man jumped down from the wall of the garden and, showing the greatest respect, told George that poverty had forced him into stealing. He then politely demanded the King's possessions.

The King gave the man his money, his watch and the buckles off his shoes, but asked if he might keep the seal which was attached to his watchchain. The man agreed to return it the next day so long as the King told no one about the incident. The thief kept his word, and the next day at the appointed hour returned the Royal Seal intact.

PETER PAN

This statue of Peter Pan, by Sir George Frampton, dates from 1912 and stands in the children's playground at the north end of Broad Walk. The original swings in the playground were a gift from J. M. Barrie, Peter Pan's creator.

FACT, FICTION AND FABLE

Peter the Wild Boy

The strangest member of George I's court was Peter the Wild Boy, who was found in the woods near Hamelin in Hanover. He was thought to be about thirteen years old and walked on all fours, climbed trees with the agility of a squirrel, and ate grass and moss.

Peter was presented to the King, who brought him back to England where he was exhibited as a curiosity and allowed to roam free in Kensington Gardens. Although all attempts to civilise Peter failed, he outlived the King by nearly sixty years.

HAMPTON COURT

Hampton Court Palace is one of the most picturesque of all royal residences, but its history is tainted by the way

in which it was acquired by Henry VIII. Although Hampton Court's story is dominated by the Tudors,

the palace continued to be a royal residence until George III, and various monarchs have left their mark here,

most significantly William and Mary.

The story of Hampton Court is most closely linked with Richmond, for Hampton's gain was Richmond's loss.

The old royal palace which stood at Richmond since the 1360s was effectively abandoned after

Hampton Court was acquired, yet the royal connections with the area have continued to the present day.

The royal park is the most visible illustration of the Crown's influence here, but there are several other areas,

including Marble Hill and the King's Observatory, with curious stories to be told.

HAMPTON COURT PALACE

A Brief History

13th century
Hampton Court has relatively modest origins. It was a manor used as an administrative base by the Knights Hospitallers of St John of Jerusalem, who also used it to store supplies for their crusades to the Holy Land.

1514
A succession of manor houses followed, until the lease was bought in 1514 by Thomas Wolsey. Wolsey embarked on a vast new country residence on the site of the existing manor, and as his power and influence grew as Cardinal and Lord Chancellor of England, so his house took on the proportions of a palace. His household became larger even than the King's, with over 500 people, rooms for 280 guests, and entertainments and hospitality which were the wonder of Europe. The King was prompted to ask Wolsey why he had built a residence which outshone his own Richmond Palace nearby, to which Wolsey reputedly replied, 'To show how noble a place a subject may offer his sovereign.' Prophetic words.

1529
In 1529, Wolsey fell from favour and was stripped of office. In an endeavour to placate the King, he offered Hampton Court to Henry, but his lands and property, including Hampton Court, were confiscated.

Henry then spent £62,000 on extending the palace at Hampton Court (the equivalent of about £18 million today). He added the Great Hall and a new court on the site of the present Fountain Court, as well as remodelling the Chapel Royal and the Clock Court. He also took an interest in the gardens and park.

1532
Henry built the first covered tennis court at Hampton Court in 1532. Real tennis had been played in England since the 14th century, predating lawn tennis by almost 600 years. By Henry's time it was extremely popular, second only to hunting and jousting.

1540
The Astronomical Clock was made for Henry in 1540 by Nicholas Oursian. As well as showing the hour, month and day, the clock also shows the number of days since the beginning of the year, the phases of the moon, and the time of high tide at London Bridge. The clock was built before the discoveries of Galileo, so the sun on the clock face revolves around the earth.

1689–1701
Hampton Court was used by Mary I, Elizabeth I, James I and Charles I (who was imprisoned there but escaped during the Civil War) but, although Charles I made alterations to the grounds, little further building was done until the reign of William and Mary, who came to the throne in 1689. They commissioned Sir Christopher Wren to redesign the palace with duplicate sets of apartments. Henry VIII's State Apartments were pulled down, four new ranges in French Renaissance style were built round the Fountain Court, and Wren again remodelled the Clock Court. Artists such as Grinling Gibbons, Jean Tijou and Louis Laguerre were commissioned to adorn the palace and its grounds.

1702–1727
Work continued under Queen Anne and George I.

1727–
George II, the last monarch to live at Hampton Court, refurbished the royal apartments and added some for his queen, Caroline. After Caroline's death, much of the palace was made into grace and favour apartments for the widows of peers and distinguished public servants; in the words of William IV, it became 'the quality poorhouse'. Past residents of grace and favour apartments include Lady Baden-Powell and the daughter of Alexander III, Emperor of Russia.

1770
George III hated Hampton Court because he said that it reminded him of the family quarrels of his youth. When fire broke out in 1770 he was reputed to have said that he would have been glad for it to burn to the ground.

18th–20th centuries
George IV, William IV and Queen Victoria all took an interest in the palace, but under Victoria the administration of the palace was transferred from the Crown to the government. The palace and its grounds are now in the hands of English Heritage and are open to the public.

Hampton Court Palace lies on a bend of the river Thames, some 15 miles south-west of the City of London. It is the grandest Tudor house in England and was one of the favourite palaces of Henry VIII, who by the end of his reign owned over 60 residences – more than any other monarch before or since.

HENRY VIII AT HAMPTON COURT

When Henry took over Hampton Court from Cardinal Wolsey, he made it his first task to remove all traces of Wolsey's ownership. Labourers worked by torchlight throughout the night until the work was completed, even defacing Wolsey's prominent coat-of-arms above the entrance to the palace.

Henry entertained lavishly at Hampton Court. In August 1546 he hosted the French ambassador, with the ambassador's retinue of 200 gentlemen, and 1,300 members of his own court; for six days the palace was surrounded by gold and velvet tents which housed the guests.

The event was not an unusual one, and to meet these demands the palace kitchens were divided into fifteen departments to oversee the royal menu. Henry built new wine cellars to store the 600 barrels of wine and ale which the court would consume during the year. Meals were served and eaten in the Great Hall and on feast days would consist of up to ten courses of meats, fish, pastries, breads and desserts. Special tapestries were hung in the hall and there would be lavish after-dinner entertainment.

Hampton Court was home to five of Henry's wives, and he spent three of his six honeymoons there, including that with Anne

The south façade of the King's State Apartments looking across the Privy Garden. The gardens were restored between 1991 and 1995.

Boleyn, after whom the gateway takes its name. Henry had their entwined initials carved throughout the palace and on many of the ceilings. When Anne fell from grace and was executed, the initials were rapidly changed to a 'J' for Jane Seymour. But the work was undertaken with haste; many were missed and in places the initials of Henry and Anne remain inseparable to this day.

Jane Seymour gave Henry his much wanted son and heir. Edward VI was born at Hampton Court and christened in the chapel with great pomp and ceremony, but only a few days later Jane Seymour died, following complications with the birth, and the joyful celebrations were brought to an abrupt halt.

Henry and Catherine Howard were married in a quiet ceremony at Hampton Court on 28 July 1540. She seemed to have a good effect on the King and for a while he regained the vigour of his youth. Unfortunately, Catherine still kept her old lovers, and reports reached Henry that Thomas Culpeper was being smuggled into the Queen's apartments. In 1541 a public declaration of her infidelity was made in the Great Watching Chamber, Catherine's household was dismissed, and she was imprisoned in the palace.

Catherine felt that if she could only talk to Henry she would be able to persuade him of her honour, but she was kept from seeing him. However, she was familiar with his routine and knew when he would be in the chapel, which was only a short distance from where she was being held. She broke away from her guards and ran to the chapel where she hammered at the door, pleading with the King to let her in. But the door stayed firmly shut,

and the guards dragged her screaming back to her quarters.

The next time that Catherine left her rooms was to start the journey to the Tower and execution. She was beheaded on 13 February 1542 at the age of only twenty. It is said that her shrieks can still be heard echoing through the Haunted Gallery.

FACT, FICTION AND FABLE

The Ghost of Sibell Penn

When Jane Seymour died after giving birth to Edward VI at Hampton Court, the infant prince was nursed by Sibell Penn, who later died of smallpox and was buried in Hampton church. In 1829 the church was demolished and her tomb disturbed. Immediately afterwards, strange noises were heard in the south-west wing of the palace, which sounded like someone spinning.

A wall was demolished and an unknown room was discovered, in which there was an old spinning wheel; the oak boards were worn away where the treadle hit the floor. It is said that when her tomb was desecrated, Sibell returned to the room which she had occupied during her life, and she has been sighted many times since.

FOUNTAIN COURT
*This replaced Henry VIII's courtyard. It was one of the few aspects of the palace completed as
William and Mary wished; financial constraints compromised their grandiose plans.*

KING'S STAIRCASE
Edward Wessex on the King's Staircase at Hampton Court, part of the King's State Apartments.
The painting is by Antonio Verrio, who died at Hampton Court in 1707.

WILLIAM AND MARY

Mary was the daughter of James II, Charles II's brother. James had converted to Catholicism and his lack of diplomacy in trying to restore equal rights for Catholics earned him many enemies. The country would probably have tolerated James, knowing that his daughters were both Protestant, but the birth of a male heir (James Francis Edward) in June 1688 sealed his fate and prompted an invitation to James's nephew and son-in-law, William of Orange, to take the throne. William had married Mary in 1677. He set out from Holland and landed at Brixham on 5 November 1688, from where he marched on London, intent on securing the Protestant interest. James panicked and fled to France, where he lived out his days. On 28 January 1689 Parliament declared that James could be deemed to have abdicated the throne on 11 December the previous year, the day on which he had first tried to flee the country.

William was unwilling to accept the throne by right of conquest but he was also unwilling to act as regent and play second fiddle to his wife, who was directly in line to the throne. The solution, reached with Mary's support, was the unique arrangement whereby the throne was offered to them jointly. After accepting the Bill of Rights, William III and Mary II were proclaimed king and queen on 13 February 1689 and crowned at Westminster Abbey on 11 April. From then on, the power of the monarch would be limited by the powers of Parliament.

William and Mary disliked Whitehall Palace, which was draughty and bad for the King's asthma, and preferred Hampton Court. Sir Christopher Wren's work on alterations and extentions to the palace began in 1689, but five years and £113,000 later (the equivalent of £7.8 million today), the apartments were still not finished.

On 28 December 1694, Queen Mary died suddenly of smallpox at the age of only thirty-two. The King had a small camp bed moved into her room so that he would not have to leave her side. When Mary died, William collapsed from nervous exhaustion and locked himself away at his house on Richmond Green, devastated by his loss. Work was halted on Hampton Court, and it was three years before it was restarted.

William continued to rule alone for the next eight years. He died on 8 March 1702, some weeks after breaking his collarbone in a riding accident in the grounds of Hampton Court when his horse stumbled on a molehill and threw the King from his saddle. He retired to Kensington Palace to convalesce, and fell asleep as he sat by the open windows looking at the garden. The chill he caught as a result led to his death from pneumonia three weeks after the accident. Fastened to the King's arm by a black ribbon was a curl of Mary's hair in a locket, but it was removed and not buried with him.

Jacobites used to toast 'the little gentleman in black velvet' responsible for William's riding accident.

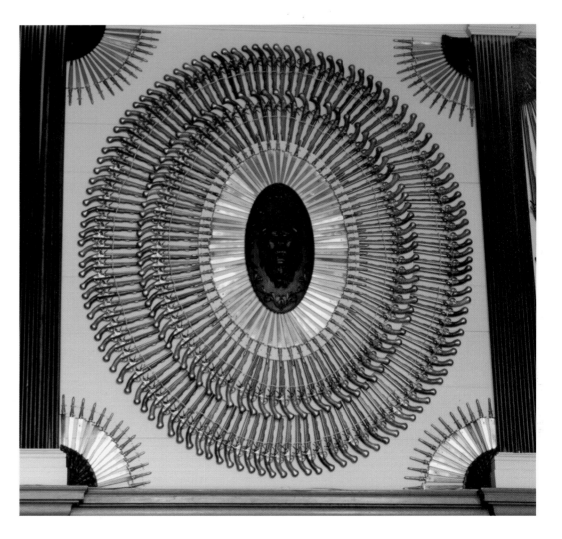

THE KING'S GUARD CHAMBER
A display of military arms which adorned the walls of the Guard Room in order to emphasise the power of the monarch.

THE TUDOR KITCHENS

Henry VIII's lavish entertainments meant that the kitchens were divided into fifteen departments to oversee the royal menu.

THE HIERARCHY OF THE COURT

The State Apartments at Hampton Court, created by Sir Christopher Wren for William and Mary, provide a fascinating insight into the social hierarchy of the court. A person's social status would determine how far into the sequence of rooms he or she was allowed to progress.

Visitors were taken first into the King's Guard Chamber; the Yeomen of the Guard kept watch here to make sure that no 'idle, mean or unknown person' was let anywhere near the King. The high walls were adorned with military arms in order to emphasise the power of the monarch, and the doors were especially large, the ceiling high and the furnishings bare, to make the visitor feel overawed.

Next in the sequence came the King's Presence Room. The throne was raised on a dais so that the King would always be physically higher than others in the room; this was particularly important to William as he was rather short in stature. Even when the King was not actually present, the courtiers would show their respect by bowing to the empty throne.

In the King's Eating Room William would sometimes dine in public. Even dining became a status symbol, with the richness and variety of food reflecting the wealth and prosperity of the monarch. The portraits in these rooms were carefully chosen to reflect William's Stuart ancestry, thus reinforcing his right to the throne.

Next came the King's Privy Chamber, which was lavishly decorated, more intimate in size, and was the principal ceremonial room of the palace.

To be granted an audience in the King's Great Bedchamber was an indication of trust and high status. This was where the King was dressed and undressed in front of the most privileged courtiers, and access was only granted by the Groom of the Stool. To show his rank, the Groom wore the key to the King's inner rooms around his neck on a bright blue ribbon.

Once the King had been seen to climb into bed and lie under the sheets, he would get out of bed and retire to the Little Bedchamber, which is where he actually slept. This ritual would then be reversed each morning.

THE PRIVY GARDEN
A view of the garden from the King's State Apartments.
William and Mary were known as 'The Gardeners of Europe'.

FACT, FICTION AND FABLE

Mary, Mary, Quite Contrary

As well as remodelling the palace and introducing lavish interiors at Hampton Court, William and Mary took great interest in the gardens (as they did at their Dutch palace, Het Loo), becoming known as the gardeners of Europe. They experimented with rare and exotic plants from all around the world, obtaining some through the Dutch trade with the East Indies and Cape of Good Hope, as well as sending collectors to the Canary Islands and Virginia to gather samples which were then kept in specially built hothouses ('stoves') at the palace.

Mary, Mary, quite contrary,
How does your garden grow?
With silver bells and cockle shells,
And pretty maids all in a row.

Legend has it that this nursery rhyme refers to the Privy Garden. 'Pretty maids all in a row' refers to the 'Hampton Court Beauties', whose portraits used to hang in a gallery at the edge of the garden and are still displayed inside the palace today.

William commissioned Jean Tijou to make the ornamental metal screen and gates between the Privy Garden and the river, and was also responsible for planting the chestnut avenue in Bushy Park as a grand new approach to the palace. He also instigated the growing of the famous Hampton Court Maze.

COMMUNICATION GALLERY
The Communication Gallery, with portraits of the 'Windsor Beauties',
representing the most beautiful women at the court of Charles II.

GEORGE II AND QUEEN CAROLINE

The last monarch to use Hampton Court as a home was George II, who added to and refurbished the palace for his queen, Caroline of Ansbach, and their eight children.

George was born in Hanover in 1683, and always spoke English with a strong German accent. He was naturalised a British subject in 1705, and married Princess Caroline at Herrenhausen later the same year. George had a preference for Hanover over England, of which on one occasion, in a fit of temper, he is reported as saying, 'the devil take the whole island'. He also questioned English manners, horses and cooking, but at his coronation on 11 October 1727 he pledged himself to the country, saying, 'I have not a drop of blood in my veins which is not English.'

The King and Queen disliked their eldest son, Frederick, Prince of Wales. The Queen was quoted as calling him 'the greatest ass, the greatest liar and the greatest beast in the whole world'. Frederick's drinking and gambling habits worsened his relationship with his parents and the final straw came when he kept his wife, Augusta's, pregnancy a secret from them.

The Queen was convinced that he could not father a healthy child and demanded to be present at the birth to ensure that a changeling was not put in its place. The Prince and Princess of Wales were staying at Hampton Court when Augusta went into labour; Frederick sneaked her away to give birth at St James's Palace. The Queen set off in hot pursuit but did not arrive in time to see the child born and was given a chilly reception when she arrived. She returned to George, saying of her son, 'I hope to God that I shall never see him again.' She died two months later without a reconciliation, although it is said that she sent a letter of forgiveness.

George II and Queen Caroline also have a connection with Richmond Lodge, which stood on the northern edge of the Old Deer Park at Richmond and is now home to the Mid Surrey Golf Club. George put much time and money into renovating the house and gardens but it was Caroline's work in the gardens that is remembered. Charles Bridgeman advised her, and William Kent designed many elaborate buildings. One of these buildings was called 'The Hermitage' and housed busts of great thinkers whom the Queen admired,

such as Isaac Newton. Another was known as 'Merlin's Cave, a grotto which doubled as a library. It had three beehive domes adorned with astrological figures and was rounded off with waxwork figures of characters associated with the great sorcerer. George had little time for these indulgences but said that he could not control how she spent her money. It transpired that it was his money she was spending: on her death it was discovered that she owed him £20,000.

CEILING OF THE CHAPEL ROYAL
Installed for Henry VIII, this fan-vaulted ceiling was carved from Windsor forest oak.

THE CHAPEL ROYAL
The chapel was built in 1514 for Cardinal Wolsey. Henry VIII's only son, Edward (later Edward VI), was baptised here on 15 October 1537.

KINGSTON-UPON-THAMES

By the time Henry VIII was installed at Hampton Court Palace, Kingston was already a busy and prosperous market town. It is the older of the two royal boroughs in London but the title was not confirmed until 1927, by George V.

A Brief History

900–79
Kingston's royal title was given in recognition of the borough's long royal history: it was at Kingston that the Saxon kings were crowned, from Edward the Elder in 900 to Aethelred the Unready in 979.

1200
King John granted Kingston its first charter in 1200 and made it officially a borough.

1219–
There has been a bridge at Kingston since at least as long as the late 12th century. In 1219 William de Coventry was appointed Master of Kingston Bridge.

1554
In 1554, the citizens of Kingston deliberately destroyed the bridge in an attempt to prevent the passage of Sir Thomas Wyatt and his followers, who were in rebellion, hoping to stop the marriage of Mary I to the King of Spain. The citizens stalled Wyatt for a few hours, which contributed towards his eventual defeat.

As a sign of gratitude, Queen Mary granted the town a charter allowing it a third fish weir and an additional fair. The importance of the trade generated by the fisheries is represented in the three salmon of the town's coat-of-arms, while the Crown indicates its royal status.

1561
Kingston Grammar School was founded by Elizabeth I in 1561.

1628
Kingston's prominence as a market town was secured in 1628 when Charles I granted a charter forbidding any other market from being held within a seven-mile radius.

KINGSTON BRIDGE

There had been a bridge at Kingston since at least as long ago as the late 12th century. The stone foundations of this wooden bridge, which were further north than the present Kingston Bridge, were discovered in 1986, during building works for a department store. There is speculation that the 12th-century bridge may have been a rebuild of an even earlier bridge, but even if this is not the case, its existence shows that by then there was enough traffic crossing the Thames at Kingston to make the bridge worthwhile.

The bridge was a great boon to trade in the town, but it also became a financial burden. In 1193 it needed repair after hostilities between Richard I and his brother John. In 1219 William de Coventry was appointed Master of Kingston Bridge and in 1223 the bridge was endowed with lands for its maintenance after damage by wind and flood. Foods again damaged the bridge in the 1250s, 60s and 80s, and by 1286 it was unusable. In 1308 Edward II ordered the bridge to be dismantled as a precaution at a time of disaffection amongst his nobles, and in 1376 it is again recorded as being out of use. Sections of the bridge were removed in times of revolt or civil war until well into the 17th century.

At some stage, tolls must have been imposed to pay for the maintenance of the bridge, because it is recorded as being made toll-free in 1565, when Robert Hammond gave further lands worth £40 for its upkeep. The Bridgewarden's accounts from the early 16th century show huge expenditure on timber, bricks, stone, gravel and iron. Until

KINGSTON BRIDGE

The present bridge was built by Edward Lappidge from 1825–8.

1750, Kingston remained the first bridge across the Thames upstream of London Bridge.

The present Kingston Bridge was built by Edward Lappidge in 1825–8, of brick faced with stone, and was opened in 1828 by the Duchess of Clarence. The Duke of Clarence later became William IV, and the Duchess became Queen Adelaide. The bridge was freed from tolls in 1871, and was widened on the upstream side in 1914.

CORONATION STONE AND CLATTERN BRIDGE

The Coronation Stone marks the place where the Saxon kings were crowned, and is thought to be the remains of the ancient throne upon which they sat, although doubts have been raised as to its authenticity. A silver coin from the reign of each king is set into the stone plinth of the Stone, which stands outside the Guildhall near the Clattern Bridge.

With one exception, all the Saxon kings were crowned at Kingston, from Edward the Elder in 900 to Aethelred the Unready in 979. This may not sound a long period, but it includes the coronations of Athelstan (925), Edmund the Magnificent (939), Eadred (946), Eadwig (956) and Edward the Martyr (975). King Edgar, who succeeded Eadwig, was crowned at Bath in 973.

The Coronation stone stands near the Clattern Bridge, which crosses the Hogsmill and is one of the oldest road bridges in England, dating back to the 12th century. It was built in stone and, although it has been widened since, the original 12th-century arches survive today. The bridge was originally called the 'Clattering Bridge' after the sound of the hooves which constantly crossed it.

COOMBE CONDUIT
Part of Henry VIII's improvements to Wolsey's water system at Hampton Court, this conduit at Kingston was securely built as a safeguard against saboteurs.

RICHMOND PALACE

The name Richmond was bestowed on the rebuilt Shene Palace by Henry VII in 1501. The palace and the town which grew up around it were named after his earldom in Yorkshire. The land surrounding the manor and town of Richmond kept its original name, which survives today as Sheen.

RICHARD II AND ANNE OF BOHEMIA

Richard II succeeded his grandfather, Edward III, in 1377 at the age of ten, and was married in 1382 at the age of fifteen to Anne of Bohemia, who was herself only sixteen. The marriage was an arranged, dynastic one but the young couple soon fell deeply in love and Shene Palace became their favourite residence. Shene was a romantic retreat and the palace a haven away from the pressure of state affairs. A summer pavilion was built on one of the eyots close by and a special barge would take the lovers across the water to their private island.

But on 7 June 1394 the Queen contracted the plague and died in Richard's arms after an illness of only a few hours. The King was heartbroken. A torchlit procession of the country's nobility escorted Anne's body from Shene Palace to Westminster for the funeral. When the Earl of Arundel arrived late and asked to be excused before the funeral was over, Richard was so outraged that he struck Arundel down with his sceptre and had him thrown into the Tower. After the funeral, the King cursed the place where Anne had died and ordered the destruction of Shene Palace, which was razed to the ground.

When Richard succeeded his grandfather, Edward III, he was too young to rule and the chief power behind the throne was Richard's uncle, John of Gaunt. The young King showed his potential when he successfully suppressed the Peasant's Revolt but his attempt to abolish parliamentary government and establish a royal autocracy proved to be his undoing. While Richard was in Ireland in 1399, John of Gaunt's son, Henry Bolingbroke, whom Richard had banished, invaded northern England and rallied enough support to force Richard's abdication. Bolingbroke became Henry IV and Richard died a prisoner in Pontefract Castle on Valentine's Day the following year.

RICHMOND PALACE
The Outer Gateway to Richmond Palace, which was once the principal access to Henry VII's palace and led directly into the Great Court.

ELIZABETH I, ROBERT DUDLEY, AND THE DEATH OF THE QUEEN

Early in her reign, Queen Elizabeth would ride to Kew from Richmond Palace to dine with Robert Dudley. One evening she was talking to some of his servants who were bearing torches to light her way home. She sang their master's praises and said that she would make him greater than any member of his family. As his father was already a duke, they took this to mean that she was going to make him king.

Gossip spread until it got back to the Queen. She brought the offenders before the Privy Council, where they pleaded guilty to 'encouraging false rumours', but the speculation did not end there. Some people said that she was already bearing Dudley's child, others that his wife, Amy Robsart, was dying from cancer and that Elizabeth was simply biding her time. When Amy Robsart died suddenly after falling downstairs and breaking her neck, it only fanned the flames of gossip.

As soon as the Queen was given news of Amy's death, she banished Dudley from the court with orders to remain at Kew until an investigation could be held. Although accidental death was recorded, the situation made it impossible for Elizabeth and Dudley ever to marry. She made him Earl of Leicester and continued to be entertained by him, but never became his wife.

In her old age, Queen Elizabeth spent more time at Richmond Palace: it had a reputation as the warmest of her palaces and she described it as 'her warm winter box to shelter her old age'. Early in 1603 she was advised by her astrologer to go to Richmond as her health was failing. But Elizabeth's health continued to deteriorate, hastened by the sudden death of her favourite Lady in Waiting, Catherine, Countess of Nottingham.

On her deathbed the countess is said to have confessed to a guilty secret to the Queen. Early in her reign, the Queen had given a ring to the Earl of Essex who was at the time one of her favourites at court; Elizabeth had told Essex to return the ring to her if ever he needed help. Years later, Essex betrayed the Queen and led a rebellion against her. He was arrested, tried and executed for treason.

The countess confessed that Essex had given her the ring while he was awaiting execution, but that her husband had forbidden her to return it to the Queen. The confession is said to have affected Elizabeth so badly that she never recovered from it. Robert Carey, the brother of the countess, came to Richmond and wrote a moving and graphic account of his time with the melancholic Queen, who died three weeks later on 24 March 1603.

For many years a story has persisted that immediately after her death the Queen's ring was dropped from the gatehouse window to Robert Carey, who was waiting below. Carey was determined to be the first to give the news of Elizabeth's death to her successor, King James VI of Scotland. On his way north, Carey fell from his horse and was badly injured, but continued his journey and arrived hobbling and bleeding. He was carried into the King's chamber, proclaimed the news and presented James with a 'blue ring from my fair lady'. Carey never stated from whom the ring came, but James took it as evidence that his message was genuine.

ROBERT DUDLEY, EARL OF LEICESTER

FACT, FICTION AND FABLE

Henrietta Howard

Henrietta Howard was mistress to George II and it was she who built Marble Hill House in Twickenham. The house was later the home of Mrs Fitzherbert, mistress and secret wife to the Prince of Wales, later George IV.

After her parents died, Henrietta was brought up by the family of the Earl of Suffolk and at the age of eighteen she married Charles Howard, the Suffolk's youngest son. Howard was a drinker and a gambler who was prone to violence and spent most of his marriage trying to get hold of Henrietta's inheritance.

It was said that even Queen Anne was nervous of Howard. Because of this, he found it difficult to win

favour at her court, so he went to Hanover to ingratiate himself with the future George I. (When it became clear that Queen Anne would not produce an heir, the 1701 Act of Succession was passed, settling the succession on George's elderly mother Sophia, from whom he would inherit the throne. In the event, Sophia died before Anne, leaving George to become the first Hanoverian king on Anne's death.) In Hanover, Howard was made Groom of the Bedchamber to George, and Henrietta was given a prominent position with the household of the future Prince and Princess of Wales. When George I came to the throne, Charles and Henrietta Howard returned to England with the new King's court.

Shortly afterwards, the King and the Prince of Wales fell out and the royal household was divided. Charles Howard stayed with the King, while Henrietta chose to stay with the Prince and Princess of Wales, glad of the enforced separation from her husband. By 1720, she had become mistress to the Prince of Wales and three years later was given a settlement with which she set about buying the land upon which to build Marble Hill House.

Henrietta trod a dangerously narrow line between pleasing her mistress (who became Queen in 1727) and her lover (now King), as well as keeping her estranged husband at bay. She did well to remain in favour, and when she was made Countess of Suffolk she was promoted at court, which gave her more time to spend at her new house. Marble Hill House soon became fashionable with the artistic and literary set of the day.

By 1734, the King was bored with Henrietta. He suspected that she was having an affair and without explanation refused to speak to her, so she handed in her resignation at court. She lived out her days at Marble Hill House and had no further contact with George II or his Queen.

Mrs Fitzherbert

In the 1780s Mrs Maria Fitzherbert lived at Marble Hill House on the Thames between Richmond and Twickenham. A Roman Catholic and twice widowed, Mrs Fitzherbert was still only twenty-seven when she was introduced to the Prince of Wales, later George IV. The Prince fell passionately in love with her and courted her with great persistence although she refused to marry him.

Her denials tormented him to such an extent that on 8 July 1784 he stabbed himself, or pretended to do so. In the face of such apparent distress, she accepted a ring from him but then fled to the Continent. He tracked her down and

bombarded her with letters imploring her to return and marry him. However, not only was she a commoner, but such a marriage was forbidden by law: if George married a Roman Catholic he would be automatically excluded from the succession, and under the Royal Marriage Act of 1772 no descendant of George II was allowed to marry under the age of twenty-five without the permission of the monarch.

The young Prince George nevertheless set about trying to find a clergyman who would marry them. Reverend Robert Burt accepted, taking the offer of £500 and the promise of future preferment. The wedding took place in the drawing room of Mrs Fitzherbert's house on the evening of 21 December 1785. Her uncle and brother signed the wedding certificate but she later removed their names for fear of recrimination. The secret marriage was illegal but accepted in the eyes of the church.

However, the marriage came to an abrupt end when the Prince was pressurised into a dynastic marriage with Caroline of Brunswick, which he was forced to accept with the promise that Parliament would pay off his debts. It is said that during the days leading up to his wedding with Caroline, he could be seen riding back and forth in front of Marble Hill House.

It is also said that Mrs Fitzherbert was at George's deathbed and that he was buried with a miniature of her, which he always wore round his neck.

RICHMOND HILL

Richmond Hill, with its spectacular views and airy position above the river became a fashionable place to live in the 18th century. There were also the Richmond Wells, a spring of iron-impregnated water that became an attraction for London society in the early part of the century, although the clientèle later deteriorated and the wells were closed down.

George III spent summers at Richmond Lodge (since demolished) while recuperating from bouts of porphyria, and would often walk up Richmond Hill to admire the views. He was also a keen amateur scientist and astronomer, and had a private observatory built for him in the Old Deer Park at Richmond by William Chambers so that he could watch the transit of Venus across the sun – due to take place on 3 June 1769.

The King also had an interest in timekeeping, and in the 1770s the observatory was used to set the official time in London at St James's Palace, Horse Guards and the Houses of Parliament.

RICHMOND PARK

Richmond Park covers 2,470 acres, is 2½ miles across, and was first enclosed in 1637 by Charles I as a hunting park for Richmond Palace and Hampton Court. It is the only London park to remain a deer park today. In 1649, after the execution of Charles I, the park was given to the City of London by the Commonwealth, in return for support in the Civil War. In 1660 the Corporation of London returned it to Charles II.

The red and fallow deer in the park today are descended from the original stocks of over 350 years ago. The gamekeepers still do their own culling and disembowelling within the park, to supply haunches of venison for the royal table and for the Archbishops of Canterbury and York.

When the park was first opened to the public, ladders were used for pedestrian access over the enclosing walls. The park gates were used only for coaches, and were kept closed at all other times in order to prevent the deer from escaping. The Ladderstile Gate commemorates John Lewis, a local brewer, who defended and won pedestrian public rights of way through the park during the reign of George II. Princess Amelia, one of George II's daughters, had been made Ranger of Richmond Park in 1751, and it soon became apparent that she was only allowing her own circle of friends into the park. The local citizens were incensed but demonstrations and petitions came to nothing until John Lewis, through the courts, successfully re-established public rights of way through the park.

The ladders were reinstated but Princess Amelia had the rungs spaced so far apart that neither children nor the elderly could use them. Lewis pushed for them to be changed and subsequently became a local hero; Princess Amelia resigned as Park Ranger.

RICHMOND PARK

The deer in Richmond Park, seen here in the snow, are descended from Charles I's original hunting stocks of over 350 years ago.

PEN PONDS IN RICHMOND PARK

THE ROYAL STAR AND GARTER HOME
*Built on the site of a grand hotel, the Royal Star and Garter Home is still used
by the Red Cross as a retirement home for disabled servicemen.*

ROYAL STAR AND GARTER HOME

At Richmond Gate, one of the main entrances to Richmond Park, stands the Royal Star and Garter Home for disabled servicemen. It takes its name from a hotel which used to stand on the site and which started life as a small inn on the main London to Portsmouth road. The inn had been built to take advantage of the view from Richmond Hill, on land leased from the Earl of Dysart. The Earl was a member of the Noble Order of the Garter, hence the name of the inn.

Through a succession of owners, the Star and Garter grew in size and prestige until one manager, Christopher Crean, gained royal patronage, which confirmed its reputation. Crean was at one time an employee of Frederick, Duke of York, the brother of George IV. The Duke stayed at Crean's hotel, and was so impressed that he presented the hotel with a magnificent silver platter adorned with the ducal arms, thus giving the hotel a royal seal of approval.

In the 19th century, the Assembly Room at the hotel became a fashionable place to hold wedding receptions; Louis Philippe stayed for six months after his flight from Paris; and Napoleon III had apartments there. The name Star and Garter became synonymous with the best standards and the height of luxury. Dickens gave a dinner for friends there every year to celebrate his wedding anniversary, and by the 1850s over 550 dinners were being served on Sundays.

In 1864 the hotel was bought by a limited company and rebuilt, to much criticism. It soon declined, and by the turn of the century was unused. In 1907 it was put up for auction and bought by the Auctioneers and Estate Agents Institute which presented it to Queen Mary, the wife of George V.

At the outbreak of the First World War, the Queen became concerned about the welfare of disabled servicemen after they left military hospitals, and so what had once been a grand hotel was pressed into service as a makeshift hospital. Queen Mary then handed it to the Red Cross, expressing a wish that it be converted into a permanent home for disabled ex-servicemen: the once grandiose ballrooms became wards, and in January 1916 the Royal Star and Garter Home opened its doors to the first 65 patients.

After the war, the former hotel proved unworkable as a hospital. It was demolished and a purpose-built home put in its place, which was opened by Queen Mary in 1924 and dedicated as the Women's Memorial to the Great War. The Royal Star and Garter home is a working home to this day, caring for the veterans of many conflicts, including some from the First World War.

THE ROYAL STAR AND GARTER HOME
Above: *A view of the Garden Terrace.*
Right: *Image of Queen Mary on the Upper Terrace.*

THE ROYAL BRITISH LEGION AND THE POPPY FACTORY

The Royal British Legion, an association of ex-servicemen, was formed in 1921 in response to the confusion and difficulties of demobilisation after the First World War. An amalgamation of various voluntary societies which had grown up during and after the war, it set up re-employment and retraining schemes for the disabled, provided funds to alleviate sickness and unemployment, and campaigned for pensions. The British Legion was given a royal charter in 1925, which was soon followed by royal patronage. During the Second World War, legionaries contributed to national and civil defence, including service as air raid wardens and in the Home Guard.

Remembrance Sunday reminds the nation annually of the sacrifice men and women in the services have made for their country, and Poppy Day, which has become one of the best known and most productive appeals in the world, continues to raise money for the work of the Royal British Legion.

The inspiration behind the poppy as an emblem of remembrance was the poem *In Flanders Field*, written by John McCrae on a scrap of paper torn from his dispatch book. Moina Michaels, an American working for the YMCA, was inspired by the poem, and in 1918 instigated the wearing of a Flanders poppy to remember those who had been killed.

Now, over 80 years on, her idea has gained worldwide momentum, and 34 million poppies a year are made at the Royal British Legion poppy factory at the foot of Richmond Hill. The factory was founded in 1922 by Major George Howson with a staff of five disabled ex-servicemen. Still run on the same principles, the factory now employs hundreds of veterans. It produces poppies, remembrance crosses and wreaths, including all those laid by the services, military associations and the royal family at the Cenotaph on Remembrance Sunday.

A CLOSER LOOK

MAIDS OF HONOUR ROW

Maids of Honour Row is a terrace of 18th-century houses on the edge of Richmond Green.

The terrace started life as lodgings for the maids of honour of George II's queen, Caroline of Ansbach.

By the 18th century, Richmond Palace was in ruins, and so the King and Queen used to stay at Richmond Lodge on the edge of the Old Park. The Lodge was too small to house the servants, so Maids of Honour Row was built to accommodate them.

Maids of Honour is also the name of a small sweet pastry which has been a speciality of Richmond for hundreds of years. Stories as to its origin abound: two suggest that the pastries were named by Henry VIII after Anne Boleyn when she was a maid of honour.

THE CENOTAPH
*The Royal British Legion poppy factory employs hundreds of veteran soldiers
and produces poppies, remembrance crosses and wreaths.*

OUTER LONDON

Parts of the country surrounding the capital also have stories to tell about their relationship with the Crown.

Just as in central London, the associations and influences vary greatly, but always reflect the changing interests of

the Crown and the people whom destiny determines should become sovereigns.

Hertford and Guildford may be on opposite sides of the city, but they share a common heritage,

both being sites for the ring of forts which William the Conqueror built around his new capital. The similarities

in their fortunes are striking, with resonances of their past continuing today. Hatfield is closely linked with

Hertford through the Tudors and is an example of one of the first royal residences that is not in fact a castle,

while St Albans is one of those places which always seems to have been at odds with the Crown.

All in all they provide a fascinating collection of stories and locations.

HERTFORD CASTLE
The Old Wall of Hertford Castle. The castle's most notorious resident was Queen Isabella, consort of Edward II,
and its most prestigious prisoner King John II of France.

St Albans

A Brief History

49 A.D.
Verulamium was established in about 49 A.D., and became the third largest city in the country. The Romans began settling the area, despite a setback in 61 when Boudicca sacked the city during the Iceni revolt.

209 A.D.
Alban was martyred.

Late 4th century
A shrine on the site of St Alban's execution was erected on the hill outside Verulamium.

793
A church replaced the shrine, and a monastery built on the slopes below.

1077–88
Paul de Caen, the 14th abbot, pulled down the remains of the Roman city and with it the Saxon abbey. Between 1077 and 1088, he built a new, Norman abbey. This was consecrated by King Henry I and Queen Matilda.

1154
Nicolas Breakspear was elected Pope in 1154 and took the name of Adrian IV. He was born near St Albans and is the only British pontiff in history. Through him, the monastery became the senior Benedictine house in England.

13th century
In the Middle Ages the abbey was extended, and became a great seat of learning. The monk Matthew Paris was appointed abbey chronicler in 1236, and is responsible for the finest chronicle of the 13th century. He also produced the first map of England.

1403–12
The townspeople engaged Thomas Wolvey to build the Curfew Tower.

1455
St Albans was the site of the first battle of the Wars of the Roses, which took place on 22 May 1455.

1539
The townspeople of St Albans were distraught at the state of the abbey after dissolution of the monasteries by Henry VIII. In 1553 they bought it from Edward VI for £400, but over the next 300 years were unable to afford the necessary repairs. Little now remains of the monastery.

1877
In 1877, the abbey was required as a cathedral, to serve the growing population of Hertford and Bedford. The tower had needed emergency repairs, the west front was a ruin, and other parts of the abbey seemed in imminent danger of collapse. Sir George Gilbert Scott began restoration work, but died in 1878, before it was completed. Lord Grimthorpe, a successful barrister and amateur architect, then stepped in; he told the diocese that he would repair the abbey at his own expense, provided it was to his design. In 1879, he totally rebuilt the Norman west front in a Victorian Gothic style, and remodelled the windows of the north and west transepts. In the process of restoring the cathedral, he added a new verb to the English language: 'to grimthorpe' is defined by the dictionary as 'to decorate lavishly but without taste'.

1882
The ensuing outcry resulted in the formation of a Society for the Protection of Ancient Monuments, led by William Morris. In 1882, the government passed the Ancient Monuments Protection Act to prevent the same kind of thing from happening elsewhere.

St Albans stands on the River Ver in Hertfordshire, close to the Roman road of Watling Street. The city and its cathedral take their name from St Alban, the first British Christian martyr, who lived in the Roman city of Verulamium.

KING JOHN AND THE MAGNA CARTA

St Albans is no stranger to rebellion. As well as Queen Boudicca's Iceni revolt of 61 A.D., and the town's part in the Peasants' Revolt of 1381, St Albans also had its part to play in the story of the Magna Carta.

King John was an unpopular and autocratic king, whose refusal to accept Stephen Langton as papal nominee for Archbishop of Canterbury antagonised Pope Innocent III. The Pope placed the kingdom under an interdict from 1208 to 1213, and excommunicated King John.

The interdict meant that church services could not take place and that marriage ceremonies could only be held in the porch and not in the church itself. King John reacted by ordering John de Cella, who was then abbot at St Albans, to hold services in the abbey. When the abbot refused, the King seized the abbey and installed his own secular officials.

This was intolerable, so the abbot agreed to pay 600 marks for the removal of the King's officials. King John insisted on 1,100 marks, which had a devastating effect on the abbey's finances. By 1213, John had alienated all classes of the community and was pushed into paying compensation to the church. A council was summoned to meet at St Albans to discuss the extent of the settlement.

Archbishop Langton took the opportunity to widen the scope of the meeting, and raised the issue of the King's mismanagement. He used a half-forgotten charter by Henry I as the basis for a document which eventually became the Magna Carta.

Two years later, on 15 June 1215, King John sealed the Magna Carta at Runnymede in Berkshire. However, he refused to acknowledge its validity and by September of the same year the country was plunged into civil war.

The value of the Magna Carta lies in the fact that it laid down standards to be observed in the future by the Crown. It also recognised rights and privileges of the barons, church and freemen, and restored the administration of justice established by Henry I. A later version was adopted by Henry III as a royalist manifesto, and in 1225 this became law.

FACT, FICTION AND FABLE

St Alban

In 209, during the Roman occupation, Alban gave shelter to a Christian priest on the run from his pagan Roman persecutors. The fugitive's prayers and vigils so impressed the pagan Alban that he accepted the Christian faith and allowed the priest to baptise him. Alban helped the visitor to escape by swapping cloaks with him. After the priest fled, Alban was arrested and taken before the town magistrates. Accused of being the priest, Alban played the part to the full, refusing to betray his new faith or to acknowledge the Roman gods. He was condemned to death and led to a place outside the city, close to where the cathedral now stands, to be scourged and beheaded. Legend has it that the executioner's eyes fell out as the sword struck.

Once Rome had accepted Christianity, and the persecution of Christians had stopped, a shrine and then a church dedicated to St Alban were built on the site of the death of the first British Christian martyr.

A CLOSER LOOK

THE CLOCK TOWER

Despite the wealth which the abbey brought to St Albans, there were often disputes between the townspeople and the abbot. As was so often the case, the abbots were effectively the feudal landlords of the town and imposed a number of petty laws which the people resented. For example, all corn from the area had to be ground in the abbot's mill at a price set by the abbot.

Similar tensions across Essex, Kent and East Anglia culminated in the Peasants' Revolt in 1381, sparked off by Richard II's third poll tax. After the King had suppressed the uprising in London, he rode to St Albans at the request of the abbot, and the ringleaders were tried, found guilty and hanged.

Ultimately, no monastic town had freedom from the church until the dissolution of the monasteries more than 150 years later. The townspeople of St Albans nevertheless tried to gain greater control of their rights and freedoms, and from 1403–12 engaged Thomas Wolvey, formerly the Royal Mason, to build a curfew tower as a demonstration of their ability to organise the town effectively. The Curfew Tower, or 'clokkehouse', at St Albans is the only medieval town belfry in England still standing. Its bell has survived nearly 600 years of use, although the frame is weak and the great bell is no longer used; the last time it rang out was for Queen Victoria's funeral in 1901.

The Clock Tower represented a political statement by the people, who used it to assert their freedom, power and wealth in the face of the Abbey. The bell gave the alarm in case of 'fire or fray' (it rang out for the First Battle of St Albans during the Wars of the Roses) and enabled the town to sound its own hours including, until 1863, the curfew. The 'angelus' was rung at 4 am to wake the apprentices, and the 'curfew' at 8 or 9 pm, when people had to return to their houses and put out their lights: the word 'curfew' is from the French *couvre feu*, meaning to cover the fires. At the curfew the gates of the town were closed.

From 1808–14, during the Napoleonic War, the Tower was used as a semaphore station; the system could send a message 110 miles to Yarmouth and receive a reply within 5 minutes on a clear day. By the 1850s the structure of the Tower had become dangerous and in 1865–6 it was restored by Sir George Gilbert Scott.

ST ALBANS ROYAL MARKET

As the number of visitors to the shrine of St Alban grew, so too did the town of St Albans and its market. The market place is first recorded in 1287 as having regular Wednesday and Saturday markets which were strictly divided into selling areas. The market was given a royal charter under Edward VI (left) in 1553.

Over the centuries, the open space of the original market place became lined with inns catering for the pilgrims coming to visit the shrine. Stalls gradually developed into more permanent stands and then into a maze of small lanes and shops, now known as the Shambles. At the far end of the Shambles (where meat and poultry were sold) was a pillory to punish wrongdoers. The pillory was demolished in 1717 and the timbers used to repair the Old Town Hall.

At the southern end of the market place the Market Cross stands where the Queen's Cross once stood. This was one of a series of crosses erected by Edward I to commemorate the resting places of his dead wife's body on its journey from Lincolnshire to Westminster Abbey (others included Banbury Cross, King's Cross and Charing Cross). Queen Eleanor had accompanied Edward on his crusades and gave birth to two of their sixteen children while abroad. Edward was heartbroken when she died. Each of the crosses erected to mark her final journey had a portrait of the Queen painted on it, so that passers-by could pray for her soul.

The steps near the cross in St Albans became a kind of 'Speaker's Corner' – unfortunately for one citizen. In 1643, during the Civil War between the King and Parliament, a High Sheriff of Hertford read out a proclamation calling for a militia to support Charles I. Oliver Cromwell happened to be standing nearby and promptly had him arrested.

FACT, FICTION AND FABLE

The Wars of the Roses

The opening battle of the first War of the Roses took place in St Albans. The name refers to the emblems of the warring factions – the red rose of the House of Lancaster and the white rose of York. Henry VI was a weak king, and at times mentally unstable. His cousin, Richard, Duke of York (a son of Edward III) had in many respects a better claim to the throne. He was made Protector during Henry's periods of collapse, and in 1455 raised a force against the King.

In May 1455, the royal standard of Henry VI was raised in the market place at St Albans; Henry had occupied the town with a force of 2,000 men. On 23 May the Yorkist forces under the Duke of York overran the town. After two and a half hours of fighting the King was captured and the royal forces routed.

St Albans was the site of another battle in 1461. This time the Yorkists were attacked and defeated by the Lancastrians, led by the redoubtable Margaret of Anjou, Henry VI's queen.

Queen Margaret fought the campaign on Henry's behalf, and it is said that

parts of St Albans are haunted in the early hours by the sound of soft footsteps and muffled voices where Margaret and her forces crept into the town to launch the surprise attack on the enemy.

The town suffered badly during and after this second battle. Since Margaret could not afford to pay her troops, she allowed them to pillage. The troops went on the rampage, looking for anything of value, even taking the jewels from the shrine of St Alban.

Henry was eventually caught and murdered in 1471, and Queen Margaret imprisoned.

When the Tudor King Henry VII came to power in 1485, after defeating Richard III at the Battle of Bosworth, the Wars of the Roses continued spasmodically until Henry finally defeated a Yorkist invasion at Stoke in 1487.

Henry claimed descent through his mother from the House of Lancaster and, determined to bring peace, order and prosperity to the country, represented his marriage to Elizabeth of York as the Union of the Roses.

The Duke of Somerset & The Castle Inn

Edmund Beaufort, 1st Duke of Somerset, was a favourite of Henry VI and wielded great power during Henry's reign. The Duke was prominent in the suppression of an uprising led by Richard, Duke of York, in 1452, a prelude to the Wars of the Roses. However, in 1454 the tables were turned; during one of Henry's periods of collapse, Richard was appointed Protector and he imprisoned Somerset in the Tower. When the King recovered his sanity, Somerset again took power while Richard fled north and gathered an army around him. Somerset also raised an army, in support of the King, and the two met in St Albans in the first battle of the Wars of the Roses.

The Duke of Somerset had been warned years earlier by a soothsayer that he would meet his end near a castle.

> What shall betide the Duke of Somerset?
> Let him shun castles:
> Safer shall he be upon the sandy plains
> Than where castles mounted stand
>   (*Henry VI*, part ii)

Fearing this prediction, Somerset stayed well away from castles, even refusing an invitation from Henry VI to attend him at Windsor Castle.

On 23 May 1455, as Yorkist troops swept through the streets of St Albans, Somerset took refuge in a small inn where he was discovered during hand-to-hand fighting. He killed four soldiers before being killed himself trying to leave the inn, where a plaque marks to this day the place of his death. The name of the tavern was the 'Castle Inn'.

Shakespeare's version is that Richard himself killed Somerset:

> So lie thou there;
> For underneath an alehouse' paltry sign,
> The Castle of St Albans, Somerset
> Hath made the wizard famous in his death.

ST ALBANS CATHEDRAL
*Edward Wessex standing by the
shrine of St Alban.*

HATFIELD HOUSE

Hatfield House is one of the finest Jacobean houses in England, and its extensive grounds include part of the magnificent formal gardens laid out by John Tradescant. The present house was built in 1607 by Sir Robert Cecil, whose descendants still live there.

THE DUAL PORTRAIT

The Dual Portrait of the 4th Earl of Salisbury and the Duke of Monmouth (below) hangs on the walls of the Grand Staircase at Hatfield House. The painting, by William Wissing (1656–87), appears to be of one man looking over the shoulder of another, but the real story is not quite so simple.

The Earl was an associate of the Duke of Monmouth, and when the Duke rebelled against James II in 1685, eventually proclaiming himself king in place of James, the Earl found himself in a difficult situation. He had a full-length portrait of the Duke in Hatfield House, and while he did not want to destroy it in case the rebellion was successful, neither could he risk being in possession of it should the rebellion fail.

The Monmouth Rising, as it is known, lasted just over a month. From his exile in Holland, the Duke of Monmouth landed in Dorset on 11 June 1685. Failing to find the support which had been promised him, he was unable to back up his declaration of political changes or his claim to the throne. He lost a decisive battle at Sedgemoor on the night of 5/6 July and his forces were routed; he was captured on 8 July and executed in London a week later.

At some point during the rebellion or shortly afterwards, the Earl of Salisbury seems to have had his own portrait painted over that of the Duke of Monmouth, rather than actually destroying his painting of the failed rebel. At the end of the 19th century, picture cleaners discovered the Duke's image beneath that of the Earl; they stripped off part of the top of the painting, revealing the Duke's head and shoulder.

THE OLD PALACE

The remaining wing of the Old Palace at Hatfield, completed in 1497.
Three other wings were demolished and the bricks used in the building of Hatfield House.
The knot garden is based on Elizabethan designs and was created in 1984 by Lady Salisbury.

HATFIELD HOUSE

Edward Wessex in the Marble Hall which was formerly used as a dining room and is the Jacobean version of the medieval Great Hall. To his right is a portrait of Mary Queen of Scots, supposedly painted a few days before her execution.

QUEEN ELIZABETH I

Princess Elizabeth spent most of the first fifteen years of her life at the palace at Hatfield, sheltered from court life and virtually under house arrest.

After the death of Henry VIII, life became more difficult for Elizabeth. Her very young half-brother, Edward VI, was on the throne, and there was considerable uncertainty over the succession. Plots and counter-plots were rife. Elizabeth came under suspicion when, at the age of fifteen, she was accused of having an affair with the Lord Admiral, Thomas Seymour, who wanted to marry her and claim the throne on her behalf. Both Elizabeth and Seymour were sent to the Tower, but the Princess was allowed to return to Hatfield to face her accusers. She claimed that the rumour had been put about to discredit her, and was exonerated; but Seymour was executed. Hatfield House still has a copy of a letter in which Elizabeth pleads her innocence and states that she is not pregnant.

While her sister Mary was on the throne, Elizabeth found herself a prisoner in the house. She tried to liven things up by holding masques and entertainments in the hall. Mary died in 1558, and Elizabeth heard the news of her accession while seated under an oak tree in the park. She immediately sent for William Cecil (the father of Robert Cecil who built the present Hatfield House), and appointed him her Chief Minister.

As queen, Elizabeth I has been variously described as 'England's most popular ruler', 'a Queen wedded to her subjects' and 'the mirror of her sex and age'. Elizabeth gave her name to the most magnificent and colourful period in English history and reigned in dazzling majesty over an exciting new age of exploration, discovery, artistic brilliance, architectural achievement and foreign conquest. Her management of her public image was faultless and she benefited from the cult of 'Gloriana' which her courtiers built up around her; she also basked in the reflected glory of the Elizabethan poets, mariners and other renaissance heroes who ornamented her long and prosperous reign.

FACT, FICTION AND FABLE

Fires at Hatfield House

Lady Emily Mary lived at Hatfield House in the late 1700s. She was the wife of James Cecil, 1st Marquess of Salisbury and Lord Chamberlain to George III. Lady Emily Mary was a beautiful, dominating and eccentric woman who would ride around the estate scattering guineas to the poor from a velvet bag. She was also a great card player and held gambling parties until dawn, by which time the floor would be ankle-deep with discarded packs. And she was still riding and waltzing at the age of eighty.

In the winter of 1835, Lady Emily Mary died tragically in a fire which broke out in her bedroom in the west wing of the house. The fire is thought to have started when her hair caught alight in the flame of a candle. Fire engines came from miles around, one from as far away as London, but were unable to put out the flames. Three events saved the building from destruction: first, two lead water tanks on the roof melted, cascading water onto the flames; second, the wind changed direction, no longer fanning the flames; and, finally, it began to snow.

Sparks were again seen at Hatfield in the time of Robert, 3rd Marquess of Salisbury, who was Prime Minister three times between 1885 and 1902. Lord Salisbury introduced the telephone and electric lighting to the house. However, the naked wires on the ceiling of the Long Gallery were apt to catch fire. The family became quite accustomed to throwing cushions to put out the flames, much to the consternation of their guests.

BROCKET HALL

A Brief History

1239–
The first record of a house on the site is in 1239, when it was owned by Simon FitzAde. In the 14th century, Sir Thomas Brocket married one of his daughters and moved into the house.

1746
The estate was sold to Sir Matthew Lamb, a successful lawyer. In 1750 the Tudor house was demolished and all that was left was the basement and cellars.
The new house was begun c. 1760, and partially finished by 1768, when Sir Matthew died.

1768
Sir Penistone Lamb (later Lord Melbourne) inherited the Hall when he was twenty-one. He completed the house, giving it splendid interiors; the saloon alone is 60 ft long and its gilt coved ceiling has magnificent and dramatic paintings of the signs of the zodiac which cost half of the overall cost of the house. The room is still intact and houses one of the world's finest collections of Chippendale furniture. Sir Penistone also laid out his own racecourse to the north and east of the house.

1805
William Lamb, 2nd Lord Melbourne, married the daughter of the Earl of Bessborough, Lady Caroline, who wrote novels and had a notorious affair with Lord Byron.

1832
In 1832, William IV appointed Lord Melbourne Prime Minister. In 1837, Melbourne brought the news to Princess Victoria that her uncle was dead and that she was to be queen. Queen Victoria often visited Brocket Hall, and every week until her marriage, Lord Melbourne sent her flowers.

1848
Lord Melbourne died at Brocket Hall in 1848 and the estate became the home of another Prime Minister, Lord Palmerston. Palmerston had been Melbourne's Foreign Secretary and, in 1839, had married Melbourne's sister, Emily Lamb.

1865
On the death of Lord Palmerston, the estate passed to the 6th Earl Cowper, Palmerston's brother-in-law, and since then has been the home of a Viceroy of India, an Admiral of the Fleet and a Scottish-born millionaire.

1892–1921
The house was rented by Lord Mount Stephen, who often entertained Queen Victoria and Edward VII at Brocket Hall. In 1921 the estate was bought by Sir Charles Nall-Cain, who later became the 1st Lord Brocket.

1939–45
The London Maternity Hospital was bombed during the Second World War and moved to Brocket Hall, where Lord Melbourne's bedroom was used as a maternity ward. The Nall-Cains moved out to Warren House, the hunting lodge in the grounds. Recently, a reunion was held of 'Brocket Babies'.

1996
The 3rd Lord Brocket leased the estate to an international consortium which now runs Brocket Hall as a conference centre and golf club.

Close to Hatfield House, along the river Lea, is Brocket Hall. When Princess Elizabeth was under house arrest at the Old Palace, she would walk along the river bank to visit John Brocket, whom she later knighted.

LADY CAROLINE LAMB

Lady Caroline married the 2nd Lord Melbourne in 1805, and moved immediately into Brocket Hall. She was a highly strung, charismatic figure, who seemed to entrance everyone that she met, yet she suffered from bouts of extreme depression. Her eccentricities verged on mental instability, and led to several nicknames: 'Ariel', 'Sprite' and 'Savage'. She wrote novels – wild, Gothic extravaganzas – and flouted the conventions. She is said on one occasion to have had herself served naked from a soup tureen for her husband's birthday.

In 1812, Lady Caroline had a passionate nine-month affair with Lord Byron, who called her his 'little volcano'. It was Lady Caroline who coined the famous description of Byron shortly after her first meeting with him: 'mad, bad and dangerous to know'. Ironically, she could well have been describing herself. When the affair ended, she spent a short time in Ireland and then returned to Brocket Hall and her long-suffering husband. Here, one day in December, she gathered the villagers to perform a bizarre ceremony. She had a huge bonfire built in the grounds; around this danced young girls dressed in white, while a band played, a page recited poetry she had written for the occasion, and Lady Caroline threw copies of Byron's letters and books into the flames.

In 1828, after a prolonged illness, exacerbated by a chance meeting with

Byron's funeral cortège, she was taken to Melbourne House in London, where she collapsed and died of exhaustion at the age of forty-three. It is said that her ghost still walks the stairs of Brocket Hall, and can occasionally be seen in the corridors and upstairs windows, or playing the piano in the morning room.

BROCKET HALL
The present building dates from 1768, but a house has stood on this spot since the early 13th century.

BROCKET HALL
Above: *The Stairwell, thought to be haunted by Lady Caroline Lamb.*
Right: *The Ballroom; the ceiling accounted for half of the overall cost of the house.*

BROCKET HALL
The Morning Room.

HERTFORD CASTLE & GUILDFORD CASTLE

A Brief History

673
Hertford was the scene of an important historical turning-point long before the existence of the castle. In 673, the bishops of the five Saxon kingdoms of England met at Hertford in what was in effect the first General Synod. It led ultimately to the domination of the Roman Christian Church over Celtic Christianity, which was a major factor in the unification of the country.

1070
Hertford Castle was built in 1070 near the site of a Saxon fort which stood at one of the few bridgeable points north of the Thames on the River Lea.

The castle motte is the only surviving part of the original Norman fort at Hertford, but in its day it was a major royal palace. Its most notorious resident was Queen Isabella, wife of Edward II, and its most prestigious prisoner King John II of France.

Guildford Castle was built slightly later. It was originally designed as a base for a band of horsemen and would have consisted of a motte topped with a wooden tower. There would have been an adjoining bailey enclosed with a wooden palisade, within which domestic buildings would be found. Its position was chosen to dominate the Saxon town.

1216
Guildford Castle was taken by the French during the constitutional wrangles sparked off by the intransigence of the English King John.

1509–47
Henry VIII was the last monarch to bring life and colour to the castle. He transformed it from a defensive fortress into a palace where his children spent much of their childhood.

When foreign policy dictated the need for coastal defences and a powerful navy, the strategic importance of the castle began to wane. Guildford Castle was eventually used as the county gaol for Surrey and Sussex, until the 17th century, when it was allowed to fall into ruin.

1603–25
Both castles were given up by the Crown during the reign of James I, and Hertford passed into private ownership.

Present day
Today, the grounds of Guildford Castle are used as a pleasure garden.

Hertford Castle and Guildford Castle are both part of what was once a chain of castles built by William the Conqueror to protect London. William chose nine strategically important sites within a day's march of London and built forts of varying sizes at each. The other castles in the chain were Windsor, Rayleigh, Berkhampstead, Tonbridge, Ongar, Rochester and Reigate.

QUEEN ISABELLA

The most notorious resident of Hertford Castle, in the early 14th century, was Edward II's wife, Queen Isabella, daughter of Philip IV of France. Such was her reputation that she was described as the 'she-wolf from France who tearest at the bowels of [her] mangled mate'. Edward was a particularly weak and inept king, utterly dominated by his unpopular adviser, Piers Gaveston, who was also rumoured to be his lover.

Five years after the disastrous Battle of Bannockburn against the Scots, Edward, now supported by new favourites, Hugh le Despenser and his son, entered into a dispute with Charles IV of France, Isabella's brother, over the lands he owned in France. Isabella was sent to France to effect a settlement, but she returned with her lover, Roger Mortimer, and others, took the King prisoner, tortured him, and eventually murdered him in Berkeley Castle in 1327. Legend has it that Isabella had Edward's heart cut out and put in a silver case. It was eventually buried with her at Greyfriars Monastery in London, where her ghost is said to haunt the churchyard to this day.

Isabella and Mortimer arranged for Hertford Castle to be conferred on Isabella for life. They crowned Isabella's fourteen-year old son as Edward III, and for three years effectively ruled the country in his name.

However, the young King took everyone by surprise by having Mortimer seized, slung into the Tower and tried by his peers. Mortimer was sentenced to death and hanged at Tyburn, having the distinction of being the first person to be executed there. Isabella was ousted from Hertford Castle and kept under constant surveillance until she returned to Edward's favour four years later. The castle was returned to her in 1331.

FACT, FICTION AND FABLE

King John II of France
Edward III used Hertford Castle as a royal prison. King John II of France was taken there after his defeat and capture at the Battle of Poitiers in 1356, but he was not kept in the dungeons. He brought with him a huge entourage, including eleven carriages of possessions, and a prefabricated chapel with all its furnishings. He was a popular figure, possibly due to his largesse: he spent £3,850 in four months at a time when the average wage was £3 a year. He was released in 1360, but, finding it impossible to raise the ransom demanded, returned to captivity and died in London in 1364.

HERTFORD CASTLE

A CLOSER LOOK

CHRIST'S HOSPITAL SCHOOL

Hertford was the home of Christ's Hospital School for some 300 years. The original school, more commonly known as The Bluecoat School because of the uniform, started life at Greyfriars in the City of London.

Greyfriars monastery was dissolved by Henry VIII in 1538, and the buildings remained empty and largely unused for 15 years. Then, in 1552, Edward VI established three royal foundations: Christ's Hospital (for children), St Thomas's Hospital (for the sick) and Bridewell (for vagabonds and rogues).

The purpose of Christ's Hospital, which included a school, was 'to take out of the streetes [of London] all fatherless children and other pooremen's children that ware not able to kepe them'.

Christ's Hospital was established in the buildings of the Greyfriars monastery, while Hertford provided an overspill for young and sick children who would benefit from healthier air away from the city.

Christ's Hospital boarding school was established in Hertford in 1682, primarily as a response to the devastating effects of the Great Plague and the Fire of London. Some 220 years later, in 1902, the boys were moved to Horsham in Sussex, and Christ's Hospital, Hertford, became exclusively a girl's school until its closure in 1985.

The main gate to the school has effigies of two Bluecoat boys, one of whom is said to have murdered the other. The guilty one supposedly looks towards the law courts, and the other towards the churchyard where he is buried. As the figures were erected in 1721 when the law courts were in the opposite direction from the guilty boy's gaze, it seems unlikely that the tale is true.

GUILDFORD CASTLE

After its strategic importance began to wane, Guildford Castle was used as the county gaol for Surrey and Sussex.
This continued until the 17th century, when the castle fell into ruin.

CONSTITUTIONAL WRANGLES

When King John (left) refused to acknowledge the validity of the Magna Carta, which he had sealed in 1215, he plunged the country into civil war. The barons who had forced him to sign it invited the French dauphin, Prince Louis (later Louis VIII), to join their cause, and Guildford Castle was captured by the French after a 25-day seige. As soon as King John died, and his nine-year-old son became Henry III, the barons turned on their supporters and drove Louis and his army out of England.

However, the constitutional problems remained unresolved. The issues arose again in the 1260s when Simon de Montfort (Henry III's brother-in-law) led a group of barons in a new bid to curb the power of the monarch; Henry III, this time with the support of Louis IX of France, had repudiated an earlier agreement transfering power to the barons. Henry was defeated at the Battle of Lewes and forced into a humiliating agreement, after which the first parliament was established.

A year later, Prince Edward, Henry III's eldest son (later Edward I), challenged one of de Montfort's followers, Adam de Gurdon, to single combat. Edward won, and de Gurdon was taken to Guildford Castle, where he was thrown down at the feet of the King. Eleanor of Castile, Edward's wife, interceded on de Gurdon's behalf and he was duly pardoned. It is thought that the whole event had been staged to encourage other rebels to surrender.

FACT, FICTION AND FABLE

THE CORNISH REBELLION

Henry VII, the first of the Tudor kings, took the crown after his victory over Richard III at the Battle of Bosworth, but his claim to the throne was only an indirect one, and others believed that they had stronger claims. One such pretender was Perkin Warbeck, who claimed to be Richard, Duke of York, the younger of the two sons of Edward IV. Warbeck raised an army in Scotland and invaded England, ineffectually laying siege to Exeter and then Taunton. Henry introduced a heavy tax on the whole country in order to defend the Crown, and Warbeck was caught, sent to the Tower, and executed.

The men of Cornwall, far from the Scottish border, objected to the tax. In 1497 they rebelled, and 3,500 men, led by Michael Joseph, marched on London, armed with pitchforks and hand-made weapons. A party of horsemen led by the Lord Chamberlain met them near Guildford and a skirmish ensued. An envoy returned to London with news of the rebel force, and the rebels continued to Blackheath. Here they were met with the full force of the army that had been assembled to fight Warbeck and the Scots. The Cornishmen retreated and their leaders were captured and suffered the traditional sentence for treason: they were hanged, drawn and quartered.

Perkin Warbeck

A CLOSER LOOK

ST MARTHA'S CHURCH

Not far from Guildford is St Martha's Church, where Stephen Langton, Archbishop of Canterbury from 1207-15, and a leading critic of King John, is said to be buried.

King John's refusal to accept Langton as Archbisop antagonised Langton's friend and former fellow student Pope Innocent III, who placed the kingdom under an interdict from 1208-13 and excommunicated King John. This meant that services could not be held in churches, and marriages could be solemnised only in church porches. The situation was untenable, and John had to make abject submission to Rome to get reinstated.

Langton sided warmly with the barons and was the first to witness the Magna Carta. When the Pope excommunicated the barons, Langton refused to publish the excommunication and was suspended from his duties.

Langton is reputed to be buried alongside a former Abbess of St Catherine's. No one knows why, although a 19th-century poet called Tupper created an elaborate tale suggesting that she was his lover before he entered the priesthood. Tupper was known for writing 'moralising commonplaces in verse' and also related what was probably already a well known local legend about King John: the story goes that King John was out hunting near Shere when he came across Emma, a woodcutter's daughter, bathing naked in Silent Pool. He tried to have his wicked way with her but she drowned rather than submit to him. As the King rode off, her brother tried to rescue her but also drowned.

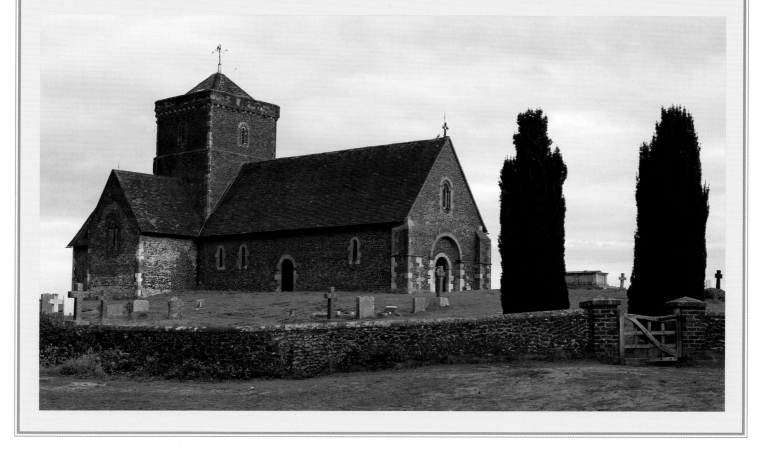

A CLOSER LOOK

SUTTON PLACE

The Sutton estate was given by Henry VIII to Sir Richard Weston in 1521, as a reward for Weston's role in setting up the famous meeting between Henry and the French king, Francis I, known as the Field of the Cloth of Gold. Weston was Henry's ambassador to the French court.

Sutton Place is one of the earliest and finest renaissance buildings in England, and was built soon after Hampton Court, in the 1520s to 1530s. An octagonal summerhouse in the magnificent gardens is of the same date as the house.

Henry's relationship with the Weston family was not, however, entirely happy. Richard Weston's son Francis, named after the French King, had grown up in the English court. Anne Boleyn thought highly of Francis and recommended him for a knighthood, but this close association with the Queen was to lead to his downfall.

When Henry decided to rid himself of Anne Boleyn, he accused her of adultery with several courtiers, including Francis Weston. The French King tried to save Francis, but Henry would not be swayed: he wanted to be free to marry Jane Seymour and to reduce the French influence in his court. Francis was executed.

CLAREMONT

Claremont, north of Guildford, is often referred to locally as 'the forgotten palace'; it was once as famous a royal residence as Sandringham or Balmoral.

Claremont is a magnificent Palladian mansion built for Clive of India. The original house on the site had been built by John Vanburgh (some of Vanburgh's work, and that of William Kent whom he employed, remains in the gardens) but Clive disliked it so intensely that he had it demolished and commissioned Capability Brown and Henry Holland to design a new one. The young John Soane also worked on the house. However, Clive never lived at Claremont; he committed suicide in 1774, and Claremont passed into public ownership before being given by the nation as a wedding present to Princess Charlotte and Prince Leopold of Saxe-Coburg in 1816.

Princess Charlotte was the only daughter of the Prince Regent, later George IV, and his wife, Caroline of Brunwick, who separated immediately after her birth. Charlotte was heir to the throne and her husband, Prince Leopold of Saxe-Coburg, was uncle to the future Queen Victoria.

Charlotte and Leopold lived a quiet and happy life at Claremont for the 18 months they were married; they took little part in society, and spent their time enjoying each other's company. In contrast to Charlotte's parents, the young couple were immensely popular, and there was considerable public interest in Charlotte's pregnancy. Tragically, after fifty hours in labour, she gave birth to a stillborn baby, and some five and a half hours later, Charlotte, too, died. The country went into mourning, and Charlotte's body was taken by torch-lit procession to Windsor, where she was buried. The succession died with her and passed to her uncle, William IV, and eventually to her cousin, Victoria.

After his wife's death, Prince Leopold divided his time between Claremont and Marlborough House, but later accepted the throne of the newly formed Belgium. From 1848 Claremont became the home of the exiled French royal family. When Leopold died, Queen Victoria erected a marble memorial to him at Christ Church, the parish church in Esher where Charlotte and Leopold attended services together.

Queen Victoria loved Claremont and was very attached to her uncle, Leopold. She spent her twenty-first birthday at Claremont, and 20 years later it became a home to her young family until the purchase of Osborne House on the Isle of Wight. After this, Claremont was seldom used, and eventually Victoria gave it to her son Leopold as a wedding present in 1882.

The house passed out of Crown hands and became a school in 1931. The room that was the scene of the tragic death of Charlotte and her baby on 6 November 1817 is now a history classroom.

CLAREMONT

Top right: *The Entrance Hall, now part of Claremont Fan Court School.*
Right: *The funeral procession of Princess Charlotte at Windsor, 19 November 1817.*

INDEX

BIBLIOGRAPHY

Butters, Shaan. *The Book of Kingston*. Baron Birch. 1995.

Cannon, John (Ed). *The Oxford Companion to British History*. Oxford University Press. 1997.

Cloake, John. *Palaces and Parks of Richmond and Kew. Volume I: The Palaces of Shene and Richmond*. Phillimore. 1995.

Cloake, John. *Palaces and Parks of Richmond and Kew. Volume II: Richmond Lodge and the Kew Palaces*. Phillimore. 1996.

Denny, Barbara. *Fulham Past*. Historical Publications Ltd. 1997.

Duncan, Andrew. *Secret London*. New Holland Press. 1998.

Edwards, David L. *The Cathedrals of Britain*. Pitkin Guides Ltd. 1989.

Field, John. *Kingdom Power and Glory, A historical guide to Westminster Abbey*. James and James (Publishers) Ltd. 1996.

Forman, Joan. *Haunted Royal Homes*. Jarrold Publishing. 2nd Edition 1992.

Glasheen, Joan. *St James's, London*. Phillimore & Co Ltd. 1987.

Hamilton, Olive and Nigel. *Royal Greenwich*. The Greenwich Bookshop. 1969.

Healey, Edna. *The Queen's House – A Social history of Buckingham Palace*. Michael Joseph in association with the Royal Collection. 1997.

Hibbert, Christopher. *London Encyclopedia*. Papermac. 1993.

Hudson, Derek. *Holland House in Kensington*. P. Davis. 1967.

Hudson, Derek. *Kensington Palace*. P. Davis. 1968.

Johnson, Paul. *A Place in History*. Omega Press in association with Thames Television.

Low, Crail and Lucy Minto (Ed). *Royal Life – Town and Country*. Handbook Publishing Ltd. 1997.

Melling, John Kennedy. *Discovering the London Guilds and Liveries*. Shire Publications Ltd. 5th edition 1995.

Milne, Gustav. *The Great Fire of London*. Historical Publications Ltd. Reprinted 1990.

Whinney, Margaret. *Wren*. Thames and Hudson.

Wickham, D.E. *Discovering Kings and Queens*. Shire Publishing Ltd. 1996.

Williamson, David. *Brewer's British Royalty*. Cassell. 1996.

Wittich, John. *London Villages*. Shire Publications Ltd. 3rd edition with additional material 1992.

Wittich, John and Ron Phillips. *Discovering Off-Beat Walks in London*. Shire Publishing Ltd. 6th Edition 1995.

Wright, Patricia. *The Strange History of Buckingham Palace*. Sutton Publishing Ltd. 1996.

CHRONOLOGY

Allison, Ronald and Sarah Riddell (Eds). *The Royal Encyclopedia*. Macmillan Press. 1991.

Cannon, John and Ralph Griffiths. *The Oxford Illustrated History of the British Monarchy*. Oxford University Press. 1998.

Charlton, John (Ed). *The Tower of London: its Buildings and Institutions*. HMSO. 1978.

Fraser, Antonia (Ed). *The Lives of the Kings and Queens of England*. Weidenfeld and Nicolson. 1975.

Howard, Philip. *The Royal Palaces*. Hamish Hamilton. 1970.

Jones, Edward and Christopher Woodward. *A Guide to the Architecture of London*. Weidenfeld and Nicolson. 2nd edition 1992.

Mee, Arthur. *The King's England: London North of the Thames (except the City and Westminster)*. Hodder and Stoughton. Revised edition 1972.
  Surrey. London's Southern Neighbour. Hodder and Stoughton. 1950.

Pevsner, Nikolaus. *The Buildings of England. Vol One: The Cities of London and Westminster*. Revised edition by Bridget Cherry. Penguin. 1973.

The Buildings of England. Volume Two: South. Penguin. 1974.
The Buildings of England. Volume Three: North-West. Penguin. 1991.
The Buildings of England. Middlesex. Penguin. 1951.
The Buildings of England. Hertfordshire. Penguin. 1953.
The Buildings of England. Essex. Penguin. 1954.

Pevsner, Nikolaus and Ian Nairn. *The Buildings of England, Surrey*. Revised 2nd edition by Bridget Cherry. Penguin. 1971.

Piper, David. *The Companion Guide to London*. Collins. 5th edition 1974.

Porter, Roy. *London. A Social History*. Hamish Hamilton. 1994.

Summerson, John. *Architecture in Britain 1530 to 1830*. Revised 4th edition. Penguin. 1963.

Trease, Geoffrey. *London. A Concise History*. Thames and Hudson. 1975.

Williams, Neville. *Royal Homes*. Lutterworth Press. 1971.

WEBSITES

The British Monarchy:
http://www.royal.gov.uk/palaces
Westminster Abbey:
http://www.westminster–abbey.org

TOURIST INFORMATION

Times of last admissions appear in brackets after opening hours

Albert Memorial
South Carriage Drive, Kensington
Gardens, SW7
⊖ High Street Kensington,
Knightsbridge, South Kensington

Bank of England
Bartholomew Lane, EC2
Tel: 0171 601 5545
⊖ Bank
Museum: 10.00 am–5.00 pm Mon–Fri
Closed public holidays, 1 Oct–Easter

Banqueting House
Whitehall, SWl
Tel: 0171 839 7569
⊖ Westminster, Embankment,
Charing Cross
10.00 am–5.00 pm Mon–Sat
Closed 24 Dec–2 Jan and all bank
holidays

Big Ben
Bridge Street, SWl
Tel: 0171 222 2219
⊖ Westminster
Not open to the public

Brocket Hall International Limited
Brocket Hall
Welwyn, Herts, AL9 7XG
Not open to the public

Buckingham Palace
SW1
Tel: 0171 930 4832
⊖ St James's Park, Victoria
State rooms open Aug–Sept 9.30
am–4.30 pm daily (3.30 pm)
Changing of the Queen's Guard:
telephone for details

The Royal Hospital, Chelsea
Royal Hospital Road, SW3
Tel: 0171 730 0161
⊖ Sloane Square
10.00 am–12.00 noon, 2.00 pm–4.00 pm
Mon–Sat; 2.00 pm–4.00 pm Sun
Closed bank holidays

Cleopatra's Needle
Embankment, WC2
⊖ Embankment

The Clock Tower
Market Place
St Albans
Tel: 01727 819340
≥ St Albans
Easter–Oct:10.30 am–5.00 pm Sat, Sun
and public holidays

College of Arms
Queen Victoria Street, EC4
Tel: 0171 248 2762
⊖ St Paul's, Mansion House
10.00 am–4.00 pm daily
Closed Christmas period and public
holidays

Eltham Palace
Court Yard, SE9
Tel: 0181 294 2548
≥ Eltham (15-minute walk from the
station)
Summer months: Wed, Thurs, Fri, Sun
10.00 am–6.00 pm
Winter months: 10.00 am–5.00 pm

Fishmonger's Hall
London Bridge, EC4
Tel: 0171 626 3531
⊖ Monument
Not open to the public

Fulham Palace Museum
Bishops Avenue, SW6
Tel: 0171 736 3233
⊖ Putney Bridge
Mon–Fri 2.00 pm–5.00 pm including
bank holiday Mondays

Greenwich Park, SE10
Tel: 0181 858 4422
≥ Maze Hill, Greenwich
10.00 am–5.00 pm daily (4.30 pm)

Greenwich Royal Observatory
Richmond Park
Kingston Vale, SW15
Tel: 0181 948 3209
⊖ ≥ Richmond
Oct–Mar: 7.30 am–dusk daily;
Apr–Sept: 7.00 am–dusk daily

Guildford Castle
c/o Guildford Museum
Castle Arch
Guildford, GU1 3SX
Tel: 01483 444751
≥ Guildford
10.00 am–6.00 pm daily

Guildhall
Gresham St, EC2
Tel: 0171 606 3030
⊖ St Paul's
Not open to the public

Hampton Court Palace
Surrey, KT8 9AU
Tel: 0181 781 9500
≥ Hampton Court
Summer months: 10.15 am–6.00 pm
Mon, 9.30 am–6.00 pm Tues–Sun
(5.15 pm)
Winter months: 10.15 am–4.30 pm Mon;
9.30 am–4.30 pm Tues–Sun (3.45 pm)
Closed 24–26 Dec and New Year's Day

Hatfield House
Hatfield
Herts, AL9 SNQ
Tel: 01707 262823
Mar–Sept 12 noon–4.00 pm Tues, Wed,
Thurs; 1.00 pm–5.00 pm Sat; 11.00
am–5.00 pm Sun and bank holidays

Hertford Castle
Herts, SG14 1HR
Tel: 01992 552885
≥ Hertford North, Hertford East
Telephone for opening times

Hyde Park
W2
Tel: 0171 262 5484
⊖ Hyde Park Corner, Knightsbridge,
Lancaster Gate, Marble Arch
5.00 am–midnight daily

Kensington Gardens
W8
Tel: 0171 262 5484
≥ Bayswater, High Street Kensington
Dawn–dusk daily

Kensington Palace
Kensington Palace Gdns, W2
Tel: 0171 823 9727
⊖ Lancaster Gate, South Kensington
10.00 am–6.00 pm daily
Closed Christmas week and for
exhibition installations (telephone for
details)

Lambeth Palace
Lambeth Palace Road, SE1
⊖ Vauxhall, Waterloo
Not open to the public

Mansion House
Walbrook, EC4
Tel: 0171 626 2500
◉ Bank, Mansion House
Open to the public by appointment only
(telephone for details)

Marble Arch
Park Lane, W1
◉ Marble Arch

The Monument
Monument Street, EC3
Tel: 0171 626 2717
◉ Monument
10.00 am–6.00 pm (5.40 pm) daily
Closed 25–26 Dec

Palace of Westminster
Nr Bridge Street, SWl
Tel: 0171 219 3000
◉ Westminster
House of Commons Visitors' Galleries:
2.30 pm–10.30 pm Mon & Tues;
9.30 am–2.00 pm Wed; 11.30 am–7.00
pm Thurs when house sitting
House of Lords Visitors' Galleries:
2.30 pm–10.30 pm Mon–Wed; 3.00 pm
onwards Thurs; 11.00 am onwards Fri
Both Galleries closed: Public holidays,
Summer recess, Christmas recess

Queen Boudicca
Victoria Embankment, SW1
◉ Westminster

Queen's House
Romney Road, Greenwich, SE10
Tel: 0181 858 4422
⇌ Maze Hill, Greenwich
10.00 am–5.00 pm daily (4.30 pm)
Re-opens Dec 1st 1999

Royal Albert Hall
Kensington Gore, SW7
Tel: 0171 589 3203
◉ High Street Kensington,
Knightsbridge, South Kensington
Open for performances only

Royal Exchange
EC3
Tel: 0171 623 0444
◉ Bank
Not open to the public

Royal Naval College
Greenwich, SE10
Tel: 0181 858 2154
⇌ Greenwich
10.00 am–4.30 pm daily

The Royal Star and Garter Home
Richmond Hill
Richmond
Surrey, RW10 6RR
Tel: 0181 940 3314
Not open to the public

St Albans Cathedral
Sumpter Yard
St Albans, AL1 1BY
Tel: 01727 860 780
⇌ St Albans
10.00 am–5.45 pm daily
Closed for special occasions (telephone
for details)

St Alfege's Church
Greenwich Church Street, SE10
Tel: 0181 853 0687
⇌ Greenwich
12.30–4.00 pm Mon, Wed & Fri;
9.00 am–11.00 pm Sat; 9.30 am–11.15
am Sun

St James's Palace
The Mall, SW1
◉ Green Park
Not open to the public

St Mary's Church
St Marychurch Street, SE16
Tel: 0171 231 2465
◉ Rotherhithe
8.00 am–6.00 pm daily; services 9.30 am,
6.00 pm Sun

St Paul's Cathedral
Ludgate Hill, EC4
Tel: 0171 236 4128
◉ St Paul's
8.30 am–4.00 pm Mon–Sat
Closed 25–26 Dec and Good Friday

Tower 42
Tel: 0171 877 7772
◉ Bank
Not open to the public

Tower Bridge
Tel: 0171 378 1928
◉ Tower Hill
The Tower Bridge Experience
Apr–Oct: 10.00 am–6.30 pm (5.15 pm)
daily
Nov–Mar: 9.30 am–6.00 pm (4.45 pm)
daily
Closed 24–26 Dec and 19th Jan

Tower of London
Tower Hill, EC3
Tel: 0171 709 0765
◉ Tower Hill
Apr–Oct: 9.00 am–5.00 pm Mon–Sat;
10.00 am–5.00 pm Sun
Nov–Mar: 9.00 am–4.00 pm Mon–Sat;
10.00 am–4.00 pm Sun–Mon
Closed Christmas Day, Boxing Day,
New Year's Day

Victoria & Albert Museum
Cromwell Road, SW7
Tel: 0171 938 8500
◉ South Kensington
Open: 10.00 am–5.45 pm daily
Closed 24–26 Dec

Westminster Abbey
Broad Sanctuary, SWl
Tel: 0171 222 5152
◉ Westminster
Open daily; telephone for details of
opening hours of individual features

Edward Wessex would like to thank the following for their help in the making of the television series 'Crown and Country' and in the production of the book:
Robin Bextor, Caroline Allen, Ian Harrison, Marie-Claire Walton, Emma Beckwith, Justine Randle, Alison Fletcher, Patrick Rowe, Simon Pinkerton, David Lascelles, Sam Montague, John Webster, Hamish Niven, Benedict Jackson, Catherine Pinfield, Catherine Houlihan, Neil Patience, Alex Marcou, Andy Smedley, Chrissy Smith and Emma Barker.

We would also like to thank Nigel Arch, Eric Atherton, Rosemary Bennett, Alastair Bruce, Anthony Burton, Richard Chartres – Bishop of London, John Cloake, Robert George Crouch, John Field, Michael Gainsborough, Bamber Gascoigne, Joan Glasheen, Susanne Groom, Canon John Haliburton, Victoria Herriott, William Hunt, Terry Hyatt, Dr Edward Impey, Rev. Glyn Jones, Simon Kewnes, John Keyworth, Lord Mayor Levene, Dr Kristen Lippencott, Eric Lupton, Cathy Power, Judy Pulley, John Martin Robinson, Treve Rosoman, Lyndi Telepneff, Simon Thurley, Frances Ward, Julian Watson, John Watts and Jo Wisdom.

First published in 1999 by HarperCollins*Illustrated*,
an imprint of HarperCollins*Publishers*

Text © Carlton International Media Limited 1999

CARLTON © Carlton International Media Limited 1999
Ardent © Ardent Productions Limited 1999

Carlton International Media Limited reserves the moral right to be identified as the author of this Work

Crown and Country written and researched by:
Caroline Allen, Emma Beckwith, Robin Bextor, Ian Harrison, Edward Wessex

Editor: Caroline Taylor
Designers: Helen Lewis, Julie Francis
Illustrator: Judy Stevens
Chronology: Alfred Le Maitre
Index: Susan Bosanko

A catalogue record for this book is available from the British Library

ISBN 0 00 414071 0

Origination and printing by The Bath Press.

PICTURE CREDITS
l = left; r = right
t = top; tl = top left; tr = top right;
b = bottom; bl = bottom left; br = bottom right;

© Carlton Television Limited/Mark Bourdillon:
2, 6, 10-11, 12-13, 27, 30t, 32, 36, 41l, 48, 53tl,bl, 54, 55, 58-60, 63, 64r, 66, 68, 69, 71, 73, 75, 77, 79, 81bl,br, 97, 100, 120, 121, 126, 131, 133-41, 143, 145, 148-9, 152, 153b, 154.

© Collections
Simon Hazelgrove 26, 29; Alain le Garsmeur 28; James Bartholomew 30b, 31b; Robert Hallmann 33b,117,122; Brian Shuel 37t, 39r, 76, 78; Liz Stares 39l, 111, 142, 161, 175; John Miller 42, 74, 81t, 82, 85, 95, 101, 103, 105, 109, 116, 119; Yuri Lewinski 49, 96, 178, 179t; Roger Scuton 53r; Liba Taylor 57b, 150, 151;

John Wender 72; Andy Hibbert 80; Kim Naylor 83, 113, 128; Malcolm Crowthers 86, 89-93; Nigel Hawkins 114, 129, 156, 157, 159, 160, 173, 174; John D. Beldom 125, 165; David M. Hughes 169; Roger Hunt 177.

© Hulton Getty 31t, 37b, 46br, 50t, 57tl, 64l, 67r, 99, 106, 179b.

© Tony Stone Images 33t.

© Mary Evans Picture Library 34, 35, 38, 40, 41r, 43, 46l,tr, 50b, 56, 57tr, 98, 102, 107, 162, 167, 176.

© National Maritime Museum London 45, 47, 67l.

© Royal Collection 1999, Her Majesty Queen Elizabeth II 115.

© Popperfoto 62.

By permission Richard Green 123.

© Arcaid/Robert O'Dea 130.

© By Courtesy of the National Portrait Gallery, London 146, 147.

© Royal Star & Garter Home 153t.

© Corbis/Michael Maur Sheil 155.

© The Marquess of Salisbury, Hatfield House 164.

© London Print Matters 170, 171.